The
Widening
Path

An Interpretive Record of Kiwanis

By
OREN ARNOLD

Illustrated by
FRED STEFFEN

Published by
KIWANIS INTERNATIONAL

PREFACE TO THE EIGHTH EDITION

The Widening Path first appeared in 1949. Complimentary reviews and verbal expressions, including those from magazines, schools, colleges and libraries, have established it as the foremost work on the service club movement ever published. Best of all, Kiwanians themselves have taken it to their hearts.

Such response can mean only one thing—that readers subscribe to the Kiwanis ideal and are eager to activate it in their personal lives. They stand proudly with men of good will around the world. The book is not offered as a reference "history" in the conventional sense, but as an appreciation of achievement, a precise statement of the magnificent Live-And-HELP-Live ideal and a guide for its application.

In the second, third, fourth, fifth, sixth and seventh editions, statistics were brought up to date and a few minor changes made.

This, the eighth edition, has four entirely new chapters, made necessary by the incredibly accelerating growth of human knowledge and of the Kiwanis programming to keep pace with it. This includes up-to-the-moment report on Kiwanis extension to many foreign countries, details on its Golden Anniversary celebration, and projection for activities in the organization's second fifty years.

OREN ARNOLD

NINTH EDITION
1970

KIWANIS   INTERNATIONAL
101 EAST ERIE STREET, CHICAGO, ILLINOIS

ABOUT THE AUTHOR

Oren Arnold, a Kiwanian since 1940, is past-president of his large Phoenix (Arizona) Kiwanis Club and remains active in most of its work. He also is honorary member of the Kiwanis Club in his summer home, Laguna Beach, California. In Phoenix he was voted "Man Of The Year" for outstanding community leadership, was awarded the governor's plaque "For distinguished service to Arizona," and has received many other honors. A native Texan, he was educated at Rice University, and has been a free lance author for thirty years. Nearly fifty of his books and more than 2,000 of his magazine articles have been published. He is best known to Kiwanians for his "Gong and Gavel" page of humor and commentary, which has beeen a regular feature of *The Kiwanis Magazine* since January 1950.

(Prepared by J. A. O'Reilly,
O'Reilly Talent Agency)

KIWANIS INTERNATIONAL PRESIDENTS

GEORGE F. HIXSON, Rochester, N. Y.*................................1916-18
PERRY S. PATTERSON, Chicago, Ill.*................................1918-19
HENRY J. ELLIOTT, Montreal, Quebec*................................1919-20
J. MERCER BARNETT, Birmingham, Ala.*................................1920-21
HARRY E. KARR, Baltimore, Md.*................................1921-22
GEORGE H. ROSS, Toronto, Ont.*................................1922-23
EDMUND F. ARRAS, Columbus, Ohio*................................1923-24
VICTOR M. JOHNSON, Rockford, Ill.*................................1924-25
JOHN H. MOSS, Milwaukee, Wis.*................................1925-26
RALPH A. AMERMAN, Scranton, Pa.*................................1926-27
HENRY C. HEINZ, Atlanta, Ga.*................................1927-28
O. SAM CUMMINGS, Dallas, Texas*................................1928-29
HORACE W. McDAVID, Decatur, Ill.*................................1929-30
RAYMOND M. CROSSMAN, Omaha, Neb.*................................1930-31
WILLIAM O. HARRIS, Los Angeles, Cal.*................................1931-32
CARL E. ENDICOTT, Huntington, Ind.*................................1932-33
JOSHUA L. JOHNS, Appleton, Wis.*................................1933-34
DR. WILLIAM J. CARRINGTON, Atlantic City, N. J.*................................1934-35
HARPER GATTON, Madisonville, Ky.*................................1935-36
A. COPELAND CALLEN, Urbana, Ill.*................................1936-37
F. TRAFFORD TAYLOR, K. C., St. Boniface, Man.*................................1937-38
H. G. HATFIELD, Oklahoma City, Okla.*................................1938-39
BENNETT O. KNUDSON, Albert Lea, Minn.*................................1939-40
MARK A. SMITH, Macon, Ga.*................................1940-41
CHARLES S. DONLEY, Pittsburgh, Pa.*................................1941-42
FRED G. McALISTER, Q.C., London, Ont.................................1942-43
DONALD B. RICE, Oakland, Cal.................................1943-44
BEN DEAN, Grand Rapids, Mich.*................................1944-45
HAMILTON HOLT, Macon, Ga.*................................1945-46
J. N. EMERSON, Pullman, Wash.*................................1946-47
CHARLES W. ARMSTRONG, M.D., Salisbury, N. C.*................................1947-48
J. BELMONT MOSSER, St. Marys, Pa.*................................1948-49
J. HUGH JACKSON, Palo Alto, Cal.*................................1949-50
DON H. MURDOCH, Winnipeg, Manitoba*................................1950-51
CLAUDE B. HELLMANN, Baltimore, Md.................................1951-52
WALTER J. L. RAY, Detroit, Mich.................................1952-53
DONALD T. FORSYTHE, Carthage, Ill.................................1953-54
DON E. ENGDAHL, Spokane, Wash.................................1954-55
J. A. RANEY, Indianapolis, Ind.*................................1955-56
REED C. CULP, Salt Lake City, Utah................................1956-57
H. PARK ARNOLD, Glendale, Calif.................................1957-58
KENNETH B. LOHEED, Toronto, Ontario*................................1958-59
ALBERT J. TULLY, Mobile, Ala.................................1959-60
JOSEPH O. TALLY, JR., Fayetteville, N. C.................................1960-61
I. R. WITTHUHN, Milwaukee, Wis.................................1961-62
MERLE H. TUCKER, Gallup, N. M.................................1962-63
CHARLES A. SWAIN, Cape May, N. J.................................1963-64
EDWARD B. MOYLAN, JR., Miami, Fla.................................1964-65
EDWARD C. KEEFE, Oklahoma City, Okla.................................1965-66
DR. R. GLENN REED, JR., Marietta, Ga.................................1966-67
JAMES M. MOLER, Charles Town, West Virginia................................1967-68
HAROLD M. HEIMBAUGH, Los Angeles, Calif.................................1968-69
ROBERT F. WEBER, Detroit, Mich.................................1969-70

* *Deceased*

IF YOU ARE a Kiwanian—or if you are an outsider looking at Kiwanis—you will realize that 275,000 men, meeting in groups once a week under a common ideal, can't help developing some important attitudes.

What is that common ideal?

What are the attitudes of Kiwanians toward one another, toward America and Canada and the family nations, toward mankind?

The purpose here is to point out the answers in a critical and interpretive record. Much of it is bound to be entertaining, for assuredly Kiwanians have done exciting things. Much of it will be inspiring, for even the most casual study of service activities is bound to inspire.

Here, then, is the Kiwanis philosophy of life, as developed, tested and expanded over its first fifty-two years. It is for all men everywhere; and no matter how much you may have neglected that philosophy as a pattern for action, it holds the subtle promise that you can yet rise high.

CONTENTS

Men of Good Will 1

Not for Back Scratching 16

"K" Crosses the Border 24

Growing Pains 31

The Idea Outgrows the Man 38

Districts Are Born 53

A Writing Fellow Gets a Hornet 61

"What's Good for Dad Is Good for Me" 68

"A Martin Askins Came Along" 76

Somebody Cares 92

A Town Reborn 109

"What Right to Live?" 123

Post-War Builders 132

Golden Anniversary 144

The Fabulous Sixties 164

Our Sacred Ninety Minutes 175

MEN OF GOOD WILL

ON A GOLF COURSE near Jacksonville, Florida, one afternoon four men paused after the ninth green. Henry "Hank" Davis, a manufacturer, glanced at his watch. It said 4:10.

"Include me out of the next round," Hank requested. "I have an appointment at 5 o'clock."

"Break it!" they demanded. "This is recreation time. You need escape from so much business."

"It is not a business appointment." Hank countered.

"Oh-h-h, a lady, then!"

Hank nodded, grinning.

"Very well, we'll all go!" his companions announced.

"And I'll let you!" Hank shot back. "I'd like for you to meet her anyway."

They had called his bluff, so he called theirs.

Together they departed in Hank's car, and at 5 p.m. were escorted into the lady's presence. A deputy sheriff closed the door behind them. They were in a jail cell.

"Mrs. McCoy," said Hank Davis, after the introductions, "I am here to report about your children, and these gentlemen will bear out what I have to say. The children are in the House of Friendship."

Mrs. McCoy, a mother of five, faced with a five-year prison term, looked mutely up at them. The golfers were ill at ease, and silent, too. Hank continued:

"We are deeply interested in those kids. They need to be cared for, and the House of Friendship will do it. Feed them, clothe them, give them clean beds, protect them. In due time they will have permanent homes. They may even be adopted if you permit it. In any event their future need not worry you. You must concentrate on re-building your own life."

There was more of it. More quiet, kindly counsel. Hank's three companions listened, then withdrew with him. They did no more razzing. Hank drove them around to the House of Friendship and introduced Timmy, Mary Nan, Prentice, Colleen and Violet, thin youngsters with enormous love-hungry eyes. Timmy, the eldest, would turn twelve tomorrow.

"These gentlemen," said Hank Davis firmly, "have been invited to your birthday party tomorrow, Tim. At 2 o'clock. I wanted you to meet them first. They are pretty good guys."

Hank showed his guests through the House. It is,

said he, an establishment to care for children of parents sentenced to jail, children who have no other place to go. It costs money to operate and considerably more effort to maintain, but a certain group of Jacksonville men supply both and find great pleasure in doing so.

The visit made a powerful impact on Hank's friends.

*   *   *

Recently in Albany, Georgia, which is a typical small city, a committee member in a certain group there made a report of activities.

"Gentlemen," said he, "our clinic has had an active year again. I will not take your time to give details here, but these are available when you want them. The clinic has now been in operation for twenty-five years, with a full-time nurse, and other necessary help as required. During that period more than 20,000 underprivileged children have been given medical attention that otherwise they could not have secured. Milk and clothing also are distributed in increasing quantities. With more money now available, we are expanding this service throughout the south Georgia area, which I know will please you."

No fanfare. No melodramatics or back patting. Just routine committee report of work done by this certain group.

*   *   *

A few years ago in another Georgia town that is even more typically American, Rip Van Winkle was asleep.

[3]

This Rip had been sleeping for fifty years. He was, in truth, the town itself—Cleveland. When a certain group organized there, it recognized the sleeping and literally grabbed Cleveland by the shoulder and shook it awake. It is unlikely that America offers any finer example of one group's accepting such a responsibility and seeing it through.

Ignoring the incredibly long and tedious detail necessary for such public service, here are a few of the major accomplishments:

A college was established in Cleveland.

A main highway was put through.

A motion picture theatre was opened.

Town waterworks were installed and put in operation.

Better school facilities were developed.

A new hotel was built and opened.

A bank was established.

One man, born near Cleveland, came back on a sentimental visit and saw the awakening. He was so impressed that he erected one of the nation's finest tourist courts, twenty-three units costing more than $5000 each. Next he added a dining place for $50,000; then a swimming pool and a club house. All told he put about half a million dollars into his "old home town" which the certain group there had awakened.

And how big is Cleveland, Georgia?

At the time of awakening—population 500.

*   *   *

In Sioux City, Iowa, one recent Sunday afternoon, a well-dressed, mild-mannered man of about forty-

[4]

five walked up the steps of a hospital. He was carrying a large red rosebud, just opening. Down a corridor he cautiously peered into a room, then entered, smiling.

"Hello, Carol," said he.

Miss Carol Hoff, age eleven, held out a hand. The gentleman took it, pressed it, even kissed it, then winked at Carol. "Still sweethearts, aren't we?" he teased. "No other boy cutting in on me yet?"

"Never," Carol assured him. "Not even if I get well."

"*When* I," he corrected.

"When I." And it was exalting to see the hope in her eyes.

"Not even when you get into high school and college, fall in love and get married?"

"Not even then, Uncle Rob. You will always be my sweetheart."

He knew full well that you must not present red roses to ladies without some preliminary courting. For it is not the rose that lifts the spirits, it's what goes with it, what the rose stands for, what it reminds the lady of when you are gone.

Uncle Rob was not her real uncle. Carol, an orphan, had no known kin. It wouldn't have mattered if she had. For this gentleman named Rob was one of a certain group who function every Sunday in Sioux City.

Without missing a Sunday for more than twenty-five years, this group has called on every child under twelve in each of Sioux City's hospitals, and presented a red rose. Tens of thousands of boys and girls have been cheered by this personal touch.

[5]

"I tell you, fellows," the committee chairman testified once in open meeting, "this giving of roses is the most selfish thing we do! For if the youngsters get pleasure from it, we get ten times as much." The burst of applause was endorsement.

They had discovered one of mankind's most priceless secrets.

*   *   *

Other groups of men, other individuals, have discovered that secret. In Kalispell, Montana, some of them were touched by the underprivileged children around them.

"Any child lives on food, sunshine and imagination," said their leader. "God gave Montana the sunshine. And He gave us the ability to supply the food and the imagination. Let's get going."

Up in the storybook wilderness near a beautiful lake, a Sunshine Camp took form. These men built it from the ground up—swinging the hammers and saws, doing the thinking and the mental labor as well, erecting buildings of rustic design that might well be part of a frontier town. Life for the children there each summer is pure adventure.

Nor is that an exceptional instance. Every state, and many provinces in Canada, have similar camps because of men who have discovered that priceless secret.

At a camp near Helena, a deer wandered in. Nobody shot a gun, nobody said boo. Perhaps the deer sensed a welcome—the wild things and the children of this universe have a kinship of spirit anyway. Soon he was eating food placed for him. In a few days he was eating out of little hands. And in a few weeks Mr. Buck actually had a bunk bed of his own in a cabin, and was sleeping in it every night. He knew a good thing when he found it.

At the same moment in history, Russia and Germany and Japan and inflation and taxes and all manner of troublesome things were bothering the minds of conscientious citizens. But for this certain group of men in Helena, the kids and Mr. Buck were infinitely more important. It is for such blessings that we live.

*   *   *

In Harrisonburg, Virginia, the people were not book minded. Yet there is reason to believe books are important; we are told that the emancipation of mankind began with the printed word, and that the best thinking of any period is set down in books. A group of Harrisonburg citizens agreed with that doctrine.

"We need a city library," said they, in open meeting. "But our people are not ready for it."

"Then let's educate them," their chairman suggested.

It was done. The educational campaign lasted three years—which is beyond the limits of many people's devotion to any good cause. Newspapers helped. Posters were used. Word-of-mouth publicity was employed. Then when the time was ripe, this group called a meeting of hand-picked citizens and formed a Library Association. Soon a room was rented and on November 19, 1928 the library was opened with 565 books.

Small? Humble? Most great things begin so.

Twenty years later the community, the entire county and some adjoining counties, in fact, were being served from that library. A bookmobile covered the rural area in a modern way. The state itself had come in with help. Books numbered into the many thousands. And the quiet men who started it all are still operating.

*   *   *

Lifting the cultural level of a community is always pleasant and profitable, and may take any of several forms. In La Jolla, California, a certain group established a summer theatre.

"If we are to do this work," said one committeeman, "it should be done well. We must aim high and hit where we aim."

Wherefore, they brought in first a home-town boy who had made good in the world of actors—Gregory Peck. And before the summer ended they had featured such other celebrities as Jennifer Jones, Sylvia Sidney and Joseph Cotten.

By the next summer the theatre had "hit so high" that it ran nine weeks, seven nights a week. Its star-studded casts rivaled Hollywood itself. Much money passed through the box office. But the La Jolla sponsors saw to it that all profits went to youth welfare work, including a fund to help needy boys and girls through college.

*   *   *

Now who are those men maintaining the House of Friendship in Florida, the clinic in Georgia, the

Sunshine Camps in Montana and elsewhere, the library in Virginia, and the summer theatre in California? Who awakened the sleepy town of Cleveland? Who has carried red roses to hospitals in Sioux City for twenty-five years?

More important—what has motivated those men?

They are neither a religious unit, though all churches are represented in them, nor are they a political, industrial or social unit. You, of course, will have guessed their organizational name, and you may even know that it costs each of them much time and money and effort to belong to that organization. Then how—and *why*—has it arisen on the North American scene?

For answer we must look to deep-lying factors, to influences that have caused gradual change perhaps in human nature itself. We must review the organization from its beginning and thereby acquire appreciative knowledge of a temperament that has been developing. If we do we shall find it strangely heartening, as any history is if we look into the hearts of men. But is such a study truly merited?

The truth is, you and I are now living in the most important half century since the beginning of time. It is imperative that we understand its importance. The sound, comparable almost to Gabriel's horn, that roared from New Mexico's sands in 1945, gave us, individually and collectively, the awesome responsibility of shaping human destinies for the *remainder* of time. The fact need not be frightening—it can be inspiring. If we study our course of action carefully, we as average citizens can realize how tremendous our moment in history really is.

Prophetically, perhaps in the instinctive way that animals anticipate a storm, a group of citizens began uniting soon after the start of the century—uniting for planning and encouragement and mutual help. An ideal of unselfish cooperation in citizen leadership (as distinguished from religious cooperation) was evolving. It had to be pioneered well in advance of its acute need.

Now, today, the acute need is here and the citizens are ready. The *selected* citizens. The relatively few. The capable. They are already banded, already firmly organized and operating, not for political gain or any form of exploitation, but solely to serve mankind. Theirs is the most inspiring ideal ever known, second only to the Christian ideal of which it may well be counted a part.

Kiwanians are blest with that idealism. Indeed they are the expression of it! They are not the only such expression; they are happily aware of similar greatness in other service organizations, notably Rotary, Lions, Exchange, Optimists, some larger than Kiwanis in numbers, some smaller. And Kiwanians have officially pledged themselves to continue their share of cooperation and cordiality that has always existed among these groups.

In common with all such service organizations (as with Christianity itself) Kiwanis began humbly. Nobody could have suspected the importance of a drop-in visit that Allen S. Browne made on Joseph G. Prance, merchant tailor, one hot afternoon early in August of 1914. Yet Allen was not pausing just to mop summer perspiration and to talk casually. He was driven from within, and he looked it. He had the countenance of a scholar — deeply chiseled features, high forehead that stopped abruptly in a heart-shaped hairline, nose glasses on a black ribbon, thin sensitive mouth; a man startlingly like his contemporary, Woodrow Wilson.

"I was wondering," said he to Joe Prance that day, "if we couldn't organize a few of our business and professional friends into a fraternal club, with a sick benefit feature.

Neither of those men had renown, and it was better that way, better than if they had been famous. For, in the idealism of this century, leaders appear not from the heights, but rise from modest offices, shops and homes. At the moment, Allen Browne was organizer for the Loyal Order of Moose in the State of Michigan and the Province of Ontario. Joe Prance was a merchant tailor, operating his shop at 1188 Gratiot Avenue in Detroit. But for three years Joe also had been president of a group of young business men banded for sick benefits and health and had found the going hard; he wasn't happy with his group, he was willing to listen to Allen Browne.

They talked at length — "brainstorming" it, as moderns might say. Browne left, saying he would drop in again soon. But he was delayed because he soon got a better job; he became national organizer for the Loyal Home Fraternity, a fraternal, sick and accident association with headquarters in Detroit. Even so, the thought of a brand new and better group continued to grow in his mind, and from time to time he did get back to the tailor shop to talk.

By late September, Browne was calling on other friends with his idea for a new group. Each discussion led to sharper plans. Donald A. Johnston, an insurance man, encouraged Browne and agreed to help him, but wanted more emphasis on the fraternal aspects of the new group, and less on the sick benefit features. This thought began to grow in all their minds.

Quoting from Joe Prance's own documents — "We held some meetings in my place of business and some at Ottie Robertson's law office in the Campau Building, always with just a small group of men present." The scenes are easy to imagine. Nothing was rushed, for that was not a go-go hurry-up era. Without realizing it, the "small group" of men were already enjoying the fraternization they sought, just by gathering in their exploratory meetings.

But the time came when Allen Browne tightened matters down by having some application blanks printed for membership in "The Supreme Lodge Benevolent Order Brothers." He took the first one to his friend the tailor and no doubt summarized all the advantages of joining again. Joe Prance was impressed. He listened while Browne painted a bright picture, then he picked up his pen. He filled in the date — December 7, 1914; his age — thirty-three; his address and occupation. He signed his name and handed Browne five dollars.

"I am proud to be member Number One," said Joe.

Browne called on the others who had talked with him and got more signatures and fees. Several informal conferences were held, and formal meetings were set up; the BOB group appeared to be flourishing. But in just a few days, a note of dissatisfaction crept in; it became apparent that the name Benevolent Order Brothers wasn't wholly satisfactory.

This was given serious discussion not only at meetings but when two or three of the fellows got together anywhere. "The name 'Supreme Lodge Benevolent Order Brothers' sounds a little pompous," Ottie Robertson agreed. "What do we mean by 'Supreme'? And just how 'Benevolent' are we?"

That analytical approach stirred more men to thinking, although the membership continued to grow. Christmas Season was at hand, good will was in the air although in Europe historic and tragic events were stirring, friends were meeting one another in various homes, and always the talk got around to the BOB. Most of the men agreed with Ottie Robertson's challenge of the BOB name.

Wherefore, at a meeting of the BOB in Detroit's Edelweiss Cafe that same month, the name matter was laid before the thirty-five men present. Discussion was brief.

"I move you, Mr. Chairman," one man said, "that we abandon our Benevolent Order Brothers name, and appoint a committee to select a better one."

The motion carried. In due time Allen Browne, Donald A. Johnston, George Eyster, Harry A. Young and Ottie Robertson were appointed as club-name committeemen. They asked the help of Clarence M. Burton, Detroit City Historian, in selecting something of historical significance, and after much discussion Browne reported for the committee.

"We have explored the various Indian dialects," said he, "and a phrase from the Otchipew tribe gave us a good suggestion. It is 'Nun Kee-wan-nis,' which in its broad sense means 'We enjoy trading, we find pleasure in sharing our talents.' From that your committee has coined the word *Kiwanis,* and recommends it as a name for our new club fellowship."

Kiwanis . . . Kiwanis . . . It was easy to say. It had a pleasing, even intriguing sound. Kiwanis Club . . . It was short, satisfying, promising, without the bombastic tone effected in that era by some other organization names. It was distinctive, and could readily be made distinguished.

"I like it," George Eyster spoke up. "I move we adopt it."

They were meeting this time in George's law office, on a December day in 1914. The motion was seconded and promptly carried.

The organization empowered Browne to print new application blanks and personally solicit memberships up to 500. He was to charge a five dollar fee, and keep the money for his trouble. But he couldn't run wild; he still had to sell men of known character and ability, and applications might be turned down by the directors (a rule that still holds throughout Kiwanis). Thus the "joiners" were kept out, the crass type that will join anything if a hint of personal gain is heard. Allen Browne was to restrict members to not more than four from any one kind of business or profession — four because Detroit then had four recognized business sections, and one could be taken from each. He went right to work, starting again with his friend Prance. "It's getting to be a habit, Joe," he grinned. "But I want your signature and pedigree again for a new organization."

"And my five dollars again, no doubt?" Joe made a sardonic thrust.

"Ha! I ought to charge you ten. It's going to be worth it."

Joe, smiling back, had already picked up his pen. Now he inspected Allen's new application blanks. They were unimpressive—the bombast was omitted even in the printing. They were simply small cards that had room for very little information. On the top one Joe wrote his immortal place in Kiwanis history. He was the first Kiwanian — Joseph G. Prance, merchant tailor. We know little about him today except that he was an honest man, a friendly man, an unselfish man, and a leader in his profession. But what finer type of individual could possibly have been chosen to blaze the Kiwanis trail, which the years have turned into a highway of life, traveled now by more than 5000 clubs and 265,000 business and professional leaders?

CHAPTER TWO

NOT FOR BACK SCRATCHING

OFTEN MEN ARE important pioneers without realizing it; they cannot appraise their own impelling force, or estimate the probable results of their pioneering. Columbus was disappointed, not elated, when he found a whole new world blocking his path to India. The Pilgrim Fathers hoped only to establish one quiet colony of ascetics. Cortez and Coronado, *conquistadores* seeking gold in our arid Southwest, went home embittered and shamed, little dreaming they had opened half a continent.

"If we work at this thing," Allen Browne pep-talked to his new Kiwanis club in Detroit, "perhaps we can build a membership of a thousand." Then, lest he be accused of optimism, he added, "In time."

"Doc" Reed was elected president of the group—Dr. Charles S. Reed, Grand River and Greenwood Avenues, Detroit. Ottie Robertson, 12 Campau

Building, was elected secretary. Directors were Lewis P. Straub, J. C. Hammer, George Eyster, Frederick Miller, Reed and Robertson. Yet all of this, done in December of 1914, was on a temporary basis and understood as such. The men needed time for getting acquainted and for letting their ideas jell. But committees were at work, and among them one brought in tentative "Articles of Association."

From our modern viewpoint those Articles were singularly uninspired. But they were a working basis, and as member Donald A. Johnston said, "They can always be changed as need arises." They were duly approved and signed by the temporary officers.

Don Johnston, an insurance man, had the knack of standing up and saying things. He did it graciously, smoothly. He said, for instance, that "most people already have their nights filled—(A dictum that has come echoing down the decades!)—so why don't we meet at noon?" A genial chorus of agreement answered him. Moreover, Christmas was at hand, the year was ending; they could start the New Year on a firm, official basis. Everybody agreed again.

Thus in that first week of January 1915 the first Kiwanis club held its first noon meeting in Detroit's Griswold Hotel. The hour was 12:15, as it is with most clubs today. And here, the club organization was made official. The same Don Johnston who "had nerve enough to stand on his feet and suggest good things" had already been mentioned for permanent president. On meeting day Don left himself vulnerable—he did not attend! Unable therefore to protest, he was immediately elected. Later they informed him of their selection amid much razzing—such being the custom of American men, even when they are serious at heart—and Don had to accept though he made a modest show of reluctance.

George Haas was elected vice-president, also over his protest of incapability. Ottie Robertson was made permanent secretary and treasurer—and here was officially launched that classic series of genial jibes about absconding, about failure to do this and that, which have to this day made the secretary the "goat" in virtually every Kiwanis club everywhere. Then the fellows named their official board. As directors to serve with the officers they chose Fred Miller, Carl Von Poetgen, Joe Prance, and George Eyster.

A group portrait of those first permanent officers and directors is worth studying. Dismiss the high and extremely-starched collar—a form of torture all well-dressed American males had to suffer in that period —and look more intently at the faces. "There, but for the accident of time, am I." You will surely say that, and know it is true. Don Johnston, circa 1915, is as *typical* a Kiwanis president as you could find in the United States or Canada today: a handsome, well-groomed man of forty-odd years, obviously forceful of manner, yet kindly of eye; his hair parted jauntily in the middle; a hint of a smile.

The others mirror the same men, almost uncannily, that you will see today at any Kiwanis board of directors meeting. There stands Carl Von Poetgen, erect and military looking. He has the set features of a colonel, of a man used to thinking, then seeing that his thoughts take tangible development. George Eyster's photo suggests that he was the gay youngster of the board, the smoothie, the fellow likely to be chosen to present corsages on Ladies Night. And we can bet that big Fred Miller had a sardonic sense of humor, that he usually listened a long while then tossed some gem of wisdom into the board meetings, dressed with a laugh.

That first noon meeting in the Griswold Hotel also approved the name Kiwanis and the Articles of Association. The latter were notarized and sent to the Secretary of State for a charter. On January 21, 1915, the Charter was signed and recorded by the Secretary of State. That became the official birth date of Kiwanis.

Twenty-five years later, on January 22, 1940, Kiwanians placed a bronze plaque on the Griswold Hotel, commemorating that founding of the organization.

*   *   *

That first group of Kiwanians *thought* they were impelled only by a legitimate, if somewhat selfish, urge to swap business and fellowship with one another.

"You help me and I'll help you," one member remarked, "is the way business is done nowadays."

He was wrong. Business, shrewd and intelligent business, had begun to drop that reciprocal trade idea about twenty years before. The idea was destined to live on in some men's minds for many more years, perhaps forever, but not in the minds of intelligent leaders. Another member arose to answer.

"I beg to disagree," said the second Kiwanian.

"I used to feel as you do, but I don't any more. It just doesn't make sense that we should be a tight little clique of 'back scratchers.' I happen to be an insurance man, but I have not joined this club to solicit you members, and I will not be bound to trade with you any more than with any other legitimate businessman. If our organization is that little, I want no part of it."

He was almost heretical. The others were silent for a long moment, then one by one they began to nod approval.

"I expect to have friendships here," the speaker continued, "but if we are to flourish as a club we must have a common cause beyond our own pocketbooks. We must seek the inner lift, the inspiration that comes from serving not self but humanity." It was so obviously, potently true that no one dared deny him.

That first Christmas, even before the club was officially launched, the members sought out indigent and crippled children, aided them in whatever way they could. An ideal, ancient yet long neglected, was being revitalized in America where idealism has been permitted to flourish as nowhere else in the history of man. Other men in contemporary organizations were sensing the same grandeur that those first Kiwanians felt.

Kiwanians had no official motto at charter time. Probably they had not thought of selecting one. Anyway, human nature being what it is, the men were having their troubles. Soon after charter day in January of 1915, some heedless chap began to grumble about Allen Browne.

"We have raised the initiation fee to ten dollars, and Browne gets all of it," he declared.

It was true. Browne had found the selling hard, and Browne had to eat. The ten dollars kept him going. Browne also "owned" Kiwanis, legally. Under an operational plan, considered wise at the time, he issued one share of stock in Kiwanis with each membership. It was hoped that the club could soon erect its own club house and charge enough in activity fees to make a profit and declare dividends, somewhat after the manner of modern town and country clubs where social life is the dominant motive. But the profit-making idea had run into that higher idealism; the men that Browne "sold," for the most part, were not primarily interested in the stock scheme or in the purely social aspects. Ottie Robertson tried to smooth out matters for Browne, and succeeded only in getting himself involved. Suspicions began to grow among the members.

President Don Johnston took note of the undercover talk but seemed not to think it dangerous. "It'll blow over, boys," said he genially. "Let's just keep plugging. We have a good club here and we want to make it better."

But it didn't blow over. The trouble reached a head in mid-July when 175 of the club men met at the Tuller Hotel Roof Garden. President Johnston had to be out of Detroit that day, and Vice-President Haas asked Joe Prance to preside. The "discussions" became historic.

One member made accusations against Allen Browne the organizer and Ottie Robertson the secretary. The accusations were found later to be wholly unjust; nevertheless, they touched off some tempers there in the meeting. Joe Prance has left a written record which can be read with combined amusement and sympathy:

"Everybody started talking at once, all 175 of them. [Even in this day and age, many Kiwanians have seen that same outburst on occasions!] Naturally the meeting was not only getting out of control, it was a stampede. I adjourned the meeting. When the smoke cleared away we had about fifty members left in the first Kiwanis club."

There, of course, was a crisis in the organization's progress. *Somebody* had to keep a level head. Fortunately, in such moments somebody usually does, especially where top men are involved. Don Johnston heard the news and rushed back home, distressed. He immediately began to call on the members and oil the rough spots. He approved when Allen Browne and Ottie Robertson discreetly left Detroit and went to Cleveland to organize a Kiwanis club there. He and a few others "mended fences" for weeks. "Time allows tempers to cool," Don counseled. "Let's not rush matters."

In autumn Don sent a message to all former Kiwanians. The message was on Western Union blanks. It invited the fellows to meet on the first Monday in October, and most of them came. Don presided.

"Gentlemen," said he, "I have the duty, first, of announcing the resignation of all members of the board of directors. And I will now hear nominations for a new board."

This startled everybody, but the sanity of it became apparent. Calmly, the men elected a new board composed of O. J. McQuistion, Richard B. Hewitt, Frank H. Johnson, Harry A. Young, J. H. Davis, Malcolm McKinnon and J. E. McLean.

"And now, my friends," President Don continued, "I hereby announce the resignation of your club officers, myself included. I now turn the gavel over to Dick Hewitt of your new board, who will preside for any further business you wish to transact."

With Hewitt presiding, Don himself was promptly and enthusiastically re-elected to the presidency — a tribute which he had not expected but which attests his popularity. The vote was unanimous. Moreover, Don continued to serve for two more years—an honor in Kiwanis that few presidents have enjoyed. T. C. Riceway was elected vice-president, Forrest W. Boswell, secretary, and Fred W. Morton, treasurer.

At once the new controlling board (which, of course, included the officers) faced another although minor crisis; they had an unpaid bill for the club, totaling $350 for service at the Tuller Hotel. They *could* have taxed the members, but instead the directors prorated the bill among themselves and paid it.

Thus the first year—the hardest in any infant's life—came to a happy end.

CHAPTER THREE

"K" CROSSES THE BORDER

ALLEN BROWNE was not a man to take umbrage (a phrase much favored by orators of the period) just because two or three fellows did not like him. He had intelligence enough to know that *any* man in dealing with other men is bound to make enemies.

"The thing for us to do," he said to Ottie Robertson, "is move out until the smoke clears. Why don't we try Cleveland?"

"Good idea," Ottie agreed.

Each of them had friends in Cleveland, so in July of 1915 they began contacting professional and businessmen there with their story of Kiwanis. "This new club is designed to gather only the outstanding citizens," they promised. "It will omit the usual folderol and get down to some concrete activities."

"Such as?" demanded a Dr. Joseph F. Byrne.

"Such as honest, honorable fellowship. Such as helping each other to maintain high business standards. Such as a pooling of our prestige for any public enterprise that is worthy. Such as a building of good will among competitors in business. Such as giving money help and personal encouragement to any group that needs it. Such as—"

"Hold on!" Doc Byrne lifted a hand, smiling. "I must have opened a flood gate!"

"We are serious about Kiwanis, sir," Browne and Robertson assured him.

"I believe you are. I like the way you present it."

"Do you like it well enough to join it? To help lead it?"

Doc Byrne nodded. "I do. And I can think of others who will like it."

Within a few days they had a small, select group assembled. Ed C. Forbes was chosen temporary chairman. His first act was to make the group a committee of the whole to survey the city for potential members. Success of that committee is attested now on official records which reveal that on October 19, 1915, barely ten weeks after Browne and Robertson arrived in the city, the Kiwanis Club of Cleveland was permanently organized with a roster of 135.

Almost at once the aggressive Clevelanders saw possibilities of expansion. Oscar Alexander, president of the new Cleveland club, told his board of directors that a state-wide chain of Kiwanis clubs was immediately possible.

One of the directors promptly stood up. "I endorse that," said he. "I have been giving thought to this club, its purpose, its potential. We have talked considerably of helping each other in business. That's fine, as far as it goes. But it doesn't go far enough. We are, supposedly, the leading business and professional men. We, therefore, have a great obligation to build the moral as well as the financial values of Cleveland. I think, for example, of our city's children. I hope we can begin immediately to show some interest in those who need guidance and help. We could start with a nursery school for underprivileged boys and girls. Literally there is no end of good we can do, and of benefit we ourselves can derive from doing it."

He sat down, and the applause was deafening. He looked up in some surprise; he had not realized that he was so close to the inner yearnings of decent men everywhere.

*   *   *

With two great cities already backing it—Detroit and Cleveland—Kiwanis had sufficient influence to command respect anywhere. The Clevelanders were wise enough to organize other clubs immediately. Pittsburgh came in. Then Rochester, Columbus, Lockport (New York), Dayton, St. Paul, New York City, Toledo and Cincinnati were granted charters.

Ed Forbes, secretary of that big Cleveland club, came to his club president, Oscar F. Alexander, one day early in 1916. "Oscar," he began, "the Kiwanians ought to be in one national organization, in the interest of unity and strength."

"You're right. Let's see what can be done."

After consulting other clubs, they issued written invitations to all, so that on May 18 and 19, 1916 delegates assembled in Cleveland for the first Kiwanis convention in history.

Except for size and for necessary pioneering, the pattern of that convention was not unlike the great Kiwanis assemblies today. Men came with a purpose. They had few grievances, but they had more suggestions than the presiding officers could handle. These men, remember, were the cream of the citizens from their respective towns, the men who had already demonstrated an ability to think. Each had ideas about what Kiwanis could and should do.

There was enough agreement on the various recommendations to allow the committees to function rapidly. A national constitution was written and adopted and national officers were elected for the first time. Four were nominated for the national presidency. They were George F. Hixson of Rochester, Charles D. Heald of Dayton, John B. Martin of Pittsburgh, and Richard B. Hewitt of Detroit. Hixson was elected.

*   *   *

Soon after the Cleveland convention, news of Kiwanis began to get around more than ever.

Even the newspapers were beginning to take notice. Editors of the period were prone to look with cynical eye on any group that proclaimed an unselfish idealism. They put Kiwanis under investigation.

"What's this man Browne getting out of it?" demanded one. "He is a paid organizer," President George Hixson answered, frankly. "Allen Browne is doing the educational work necessary to any growth of this sort. It takes talent to go coldly into a town and sell an intangible, especially an idea that requires men to give of their money and time and energy to humanity. True, each of us has some of that talent. But Browne is trained for it, and can accomplish more by virtue of experience. I am glad to allocate a few dollars of my club dues to supporting men like Browne."

The editor slowly nodded, "I hadn't thought of that," he admitted.

"There's this, too: If he or any other paid organizer ever appears to be taking advantage of his position, I think Kiwanis has men shrewd enough to recognize it and take the necessary action. Have you studied the *type* of men in this organization, sir?"

The press found that the men of Kiwanis were citizens of influence and position, indeed they were some of the newspapers' heaviest advertisers, and were doing an increasing amount of community service. As an organization, Kiwanis was one heartening sign of goodness in a world that was war-torn. The Kaiser had made it clear that he expected soon to rule the earth. In America men were banding together in support of doctrines directly opposite to the Kaiser's; the grandeur of Americanism was finding a quiet new expression.

Biggest single newspaper play given to Kiwanis in those formative months came not in the United States, however, but in Canada. In the autumn of 1916, A. S. Kirby, a district organizer for Kiwanis, had occasion to visit Hamilton, Ontario. The Canadians, he observed, were as conscious of community needs as were their friends south of the border. The

Canadians had heard of Kiwanis; they were pleased to listen to Kirby. By October 16 they had a temporary committee working with him, and on November 1, 1916, at noon in the Royal Connaught Hotel of Hamilton, the club was organized. Two weeks later *The Hamilton Spectator* devoted virtually all of a fourteen-page newspaper section to an exposition of Kiwanis purposes and accomplishments.

In that paper, moreover, began the gestation of the Kiwanis slogan. *The Spectator* arbitrarily suggested a starter: "For Better Business—Right Service, Right Quantity—Service Brings Its Own Reward." It was the necessarily hurried work of some reporter, and was too heavy for permanent use. Yet it had the basic thought. The Hamiltonians themselves were immediately concerned with public service. The first summer of their club's existence saw the Kiwanians voting to "offer their services for one or two days each month to farmers to help garner crops." Farm crops must not be allowed to go to waste, with a dictator threatening the world. In that same critical summer of 1917 the Hamilton club, still pioneering but on the right trail, sponsored Chautauqua meetings to help the Red Cross. (Chautauqua, if you are too young to remember, was the traveling culture of the period; the series of distinguished lecturers, musicians and entertainers brought through national circuits, often in tent theatres.) It also aided the Hamilton Baby Welfare Association that summer, worked in selling Liberty Bonds, helped care for disabled soldiers, and provided Christmas cheer for hundreds of underprivileged children.

That in its first year of existence was enough to

assure permanent distinction for the Hamilton club. It is honored to this day for being the club that made Kiwanis international.

CHAPTER FOUR

GROWING PAINS

IWANIS MOVING into Canada was like a child entering kindergarten; the growth was so rapid as to be astonishing. Before anyone quite realized it, adolescence had set in. Specifically, Kiwanis had sixteen clubs in six states when the first national convention was held at Cleveland. Next year, May 1917, the convention was in Kiwanis' birthplace, Detroit, and fifty-five clubs were in the organization, representing states from Texas to the Atlantic and including four in Canada. Already there were more than 5700 Kiwanians.

"If nothing else attests to it, the very growth of Kiwanis makes it important on the national scene," wrote one editor in his newspaper.

It must be confessed that some growing pains were felt. In one town a few noisy gents took control of the new club and promptly converted it into a weekly session of carousing. As two-thirds of its initial membership dropped out, the club died a natural and unlamented death. Six years had to pass before Kiwanis could resume its rightful, dignified place in that community.

In another club a secretary-treasurer collected dues and contributions totaling almost $1400; then one day didn't show up for meeting.

"I bet Jack has absconded," one member joshed. (Jack was not the official's real name.)

The boys all laughed, ate their cold chicken a la king, drank their coffee, heard their program, and went away. Next week, Jack was absent again. The vice-president was asked to take the roll and generally run the routine until Jack could get back.

Two months later it became known positively that good old Jack really had absconded. Yet no earthquake ensued. A simple job of detective work located Jack — down and out, shamed, broke and broken, in another state. His Kiwanis compadres quietly heard the facts, then did a characteristic thing.

"I move you, Mr. President," one member said in next meeting, "that the loan of $1400 made to our friend Jack be extended indefinitely, until he can regain his health and repay it."

Loan? . . . Friend? . . . A few men were startled; they would have turned the whole matter over to the police. Jack was in excellent physical health, they knew.

"Mr. President," another spoke up, "I second the motion. I have known Jack for sixteen years. He has been a fine citizen. Whatever happened to him might have happened to any one of us. And time, I have learned, can work miracles."

The motion passed unanimously, and Jack was so notified. At first he wouldn't believe it. He had prepared himself, in his mind, for prison. A loan? . . . From *friends?* . . . Somebody got Jack a new job. And in barely three years the $1400 was paid back to the club, plus a bonus of $2000 more! It was a high rate of interest. But heart interest, voluntarily paid on a loan of love, usually does run high.

Handling its own mistakes, then, was a part of the Kiwanis growing process. Social customs varied importantly from area to area in our vast nation. It was difficult at first to crack some conservative eastern communities without sympathetic approach. They just didn't *want* Kiwanis, felt no need of it, felt that no smooth-talking salesman like Browne could possibly have anything worthwhile. Farther west, any new idea was welcomed, sometimes too quickly, too noisily. In one western community the townsmen announced a big whoop-te-do and had everybody from the garbage collectors to the bank presidents at one big mass meeting, taking an oath of Kiwanis membership. True, all of them may have been honorable men, but at the second meeting less than half showed up. By the end of the month the original 658 "members" could be tactfully cut to eighty-seven known community leaders. In that town Kiwanis is prospering to this day.

Independence of spirit had to be faced in those formative years, just as it must be today. Such independence is a good thing; Kiwanis International encourages it. Yet, unbridled, it can run away and do much harm. "Why should we affiliate ourselves with some organization in Michigan or New York?" a western Kiwanis club demanded. Such comments, too, were heard in the South.

But all were more American than provincial, more cooperative than suspicious. Given time to let their spirits roam, they saw the common sense of being in the now very strong International organization.

Strength of the International first became apparent at the Detroit convention in 1917. It was evident in the statistics, yes, but more so in the purposeful manner with which delegates spoke and took official actions. To an outsider, it was also evident in the very faces of the men there, the types.

Most of the Kiwanians, one commentator of the period noted, were big. Big physically, or big mentally, or both. They were executive types. They could look you straight in the eye and say an emphatic but kindly yes or no and mean it. An increasing number were men who had been college trained; doctors, attorneys, judges, engineers, presidents of this and managers of that, professors, outstanding agriculturists, merchants of distinction. Most of them, inevitably, were men of financial means, yet merely being well-to-do was not emphasized. In short, it became apparent even back there in 1917 that here were the top individuals; here was a cross section not of American men but of American leadership.

At Detroit they ironed out a great many problems. Cities like New York, for instance, had been found too large for just one Kiwanis club; the potential membership couldn't possibly get into any one dining room. So, additional clubs were authorized, for the New York boroughs in that instance. Today many cities have multiple clubs, based usually on geographic divisions. Metropolitan Chicago, for instance, has thirty-two clubs at this writing, with more planned. Los Angeles embraces thirty-eight within its city limits.

At Detroit, too, the matter of dues was smoothed out. Most clubs had been collecting negligible dues, some as low as twenty-five cents a member. This had been found completely inadequate. President Hixson reported on it.

"A number of clubs have sent but one delegate to this second convention," said he, "because they lacked sufficient funds to send more. Their activities are handicapped. No businessman can afford to belong to an organization that is not on a sound business and financial basis. The per capita dues of twenty-five cents is not sufficient. It is the belief of your International Board that no organization such as this can exist on a less amount of dues than ten dollars per member."

From that moment the financial as well as the numerical and moral strength of Kiwanis International began to expand rapidly. Soon virtually every club not only made itself solvent, but built up a comfortable reserve. By mid-century some clubs had many thousands of dollars in their treasuries, not just in pride or acquisitiveness but as a backlog for service activities.

"Let no Kiwanian ever be taxed in any way that is burdensome," President Hixson pleaded in 1917. "But let every member know that he is not a true

Kiwanian if he does not have a generous heart."

The convention backed him with enthusiasm, thereby setting a policy good probably for all time. No Kiwanian today is ever burdened by excessive dues or assessments. Most club treasuries, in fact, are swelled by fund-raising activities, which aid everybody concerned.

*　　*　　*

That second International convention, held at Detroit, did two other things which time has proven memorable. One was the designing and adopting of the official emblem. Records show that delegate Andrew Snyder of Newark, New Jersey, reporting for the Constitutional Committee, announced: "Your Committee moves the adoption of the following: Be it resolved that this convention assembled adopt as an official emblem the letter 'K' surrounded by the words 'Kiwanis Club' within a double circle."

With slight change, that is the official emblem used today. The word "Club" in the double circle has been changed to "International," and a rope surrounds the larger circle. Done in blue and gold, the emblem is more than an accurate label and symbol; it is a design of exquisite simplicity, lending itself admirably to banners, jewelry, or wherever an imprint is desired.

The other, and even more important, resolution adopted at Detroit was a declaration of patriotism.

No declaration, as such, was needed; nobody had questioned Kiwanians' patriotism, not even inferentially. Nevertheless, on the world horizon at that moment was the darkest cloud since 1860; human liberty was threatened. Some strong, unequivocal re-statement of our determination to guard that liberty was appropriate; Kiwanians *wanted* to make such a statement, wanted to reveal the two most cherished ideals in their hearts—love of God and love of country. President Hixson appointed a committee to phrase the resolution. It included Loren E. Sowers of Canton, Ohio; R. W. Thompson of Hartford, Connecticut; and H. J. Hale of Hamilton, Ontario.

The actual wording of their resolution, adopted unanimously and with enthusiasm, was not distinguished, perhaps because the committeemen were not given to "fine writing." Nevertheless its meaning was unmistakable, its challenge clear, its strength as evident as is any resolution today when Kiwanis International in convention backs any policy for human welfare. The Kaiser had a "Big Bertha" gun, with a range of seventy-five miles. America had a new spiritual gun of such range that it has been roaring around the earth to this day and will so roar forever. The *voluntarily* organized business leaders of America, as seen in Kiwanis and other service groups of equal distinction, were perhaps the most powerful single force in overthrowing the dictators of 1918 and 1945. They are even more powerful against any dictators now or hereafter.

Through them let liberty-loving people everywhere maintain hope.

CHAPTER FIVE

THE IDEA OUTGROWS THE MAN

ERE, then, was a lusty youth, growing in vigor and influence beyond all predictions. Fifty-five clubs reporting at the 1917 convention in Detroit was considered astonishing. But in June 1918 at the Providence convention, the clubs had grown to ninety-three and many more were a-borning. Kiwanians pointed with pride. Orators orated about it. Opportunists tried to make something of the situation for themselves — would Kiwanis endorse this, that, or the other? — would Kiwanis like to buy 10,000 banners to give its members? (At two dollars each for a thirty-cent banner, this chap would have made a killing.) Would Kiwanis accept a donation of say $5000 for its International treasury from the Honorable Joe Doakes, who just happens to be running for a high political office?

"It is becoming apparent," said one leader, "that we have too little coordination of ideas. Kiwanis will have a thousand faces if something isn't done."

No strong central organization had developed, and none seemed feasible at the moment. But other conscientious men had been thinking, too. One of them, Perry Patterson of Chicago, came before the convention at Providence with a suggestion.

"Our greatest difficulty," said he, "is maintaining close contact and communication among the individual clubs. Therefore, I recommend that Kiwanis be organized into districts, so that frequent conferences can be held. Problems peculiar to one district often are not found elsewhere, and the conferences can solve these problems on the basis of regional need. Permanent organizations could be set up, with district governors elected. Then these district governors could become the trustees of the International organization, in much the same way that senators and representatives compose the Congress in our national government."

Convention delegates began buzzing in approval. L. M. Hammerschmidt of South Bend, Indiana was presiding that morning. He let the buzzing go on for a few minutes, then recognized delegates one by one who arose to endorse Perry Patterson's suggestion. Next he gave the floor to Daniel S. Wentworth of Chicago.

"Mr. Chairman and friends," Dan began, "at first blush, the suggestion of Mr. Patterson seems excellent. But on more careful consideration I think you will find it not so good.

"I say let the districts be organized, surely; and

let them treat with the clubs and members geographically. But let our International trustees represent us on a per capita basis. Trustees must not see geographic boundaries; they must see men banded together for service. They must not focus attention on regional ideas, but on ideas that affect whole nations and all of mankind. A district governor, ever so capable regionally, might not have had the opportunity, the training, the wisdom, to serve us as an International trustee."

He sat down, and there was another kind of buzzing. He had truly shown the other side—the one that lurks invariably around back of every question. Yet some couldn't see it. They stood up to restate their side. Chairman Hammerschmidt encouraged both groups to speak, and there was no reticence. Eventually the matter came to a vote, and while the convention approved the thought of organizing Kiwanis into districts with elected district governors, it decided fifty-one to thirty-seven against allowing the governors to be *ipso facto* International trustees.

Time has proved both arrangements to be good ones.

*   *   *

At the 1918 convention in Providence, it was apparent that an awkward situation had developed. Kiwanis, already a vast organization, was owned body and soul by one man!

"I don't like it," a delegate said frankly.

Others echoed him. Yet none could say precisely why. When they stood up in meeting they were guilty of circumlocution. Even at recess periods they simply puffed cigars a little harder, grimaced a bit more fiercely, and said the same generalities a little louder. But the sum of it all was, they resented being "under the thumb" of one man. The man was, of course, Allen Browne, the chap who conceived Kiwanis in the first place, and who was still its national organizer.

Detailed study of the records and probing of memories show that Allen can be accused of almost nothing except enthusiasm. Nevertheless, male nature is such that it frets under any kind of one-man dominance; Americans and Canadians just have to rule themselves, or think they rule themselves, in order to be content. They will let their own elected politicians exploit them, but will shout to high heaven and roll up their sleeves if they discover they lack the power to evict those politicians.

Suddenly it dawned on the Kiwanians that they lacked the power to evict Allen Browne. Unmistakably he was a "politician," that is he was political, diplomatic, aggressive, ambitious. He was making a good thing of Kiwanis for himself, financially; doubtless much better than even he had dreamed of. Wherefore, at Providence some of the loudest bickering ever heard in convention was aimed at him. But, as usual in such a crisis, a level-headed leader calmly stepped up and took charge. He was a man with a high sense of humor who announced that "Ah represent one of the othuh nations in Kiwanis International."

"You mean you're from Canada?" some innocent asked.

"No suh, from Take-sus."

Orville Thorp from deep Dallas, then, was the man who stood up smiling, to tell the boys to stop all this growling about organizer Browne and let's get at the heart of the matter.

"If he's guilty," Orville said, dropping his drawl now, "we shall determine that and take proper action. If he isn't we must apologize, shake his hand and send him forth with our heartiest endorsement. Why, gentlemen, we don't hang a man without a fair hearing even in Texas!"

Thus the Dallas psychology worked. The organization might have disintegrated in disgust right there, after having done a grave injustice. But it didn't. Allen Browne's contract with Kiwanis was coolly and calmly brought up for committee study. It was found to have some faults. Even Browne admitted them. So the committee devised a now famous new contract which it awarded him.

Over the decades a surprising interest has been shown in that contract—a continuing interest—perhaps because Kiwanis has so many distinguished lawyers and judges. It *is* interesting, even strange, that a renewed contract should have been given to Browne at all, considering that it still allowed him to "own" Kiwanis. Yet it was by no means one-sided, nor vicious in any degree.

Here is the way the contract read:

This agreement made this twenty-eighth day of June, 1918, by and between the Kiwanis Club, an Ohio Corporation as party of the first part, and Allen S. Browne of Erie, New York, party of the second part

WITNESSETH

The parties hereby having herebefore on the sixth day of

November, 1915 made and entered into an agreement in writing that they now desire to revoke, annul and rescind and to make and execute this contract in place thereof

NOW, THEREFORE in consideration of the sum of one dollar and other mutual covenants, agreements and promises of the parties hereto it is agreed

First—that the party of the first part employs said Browne as International Organizer of Kiwanis clubs under the following terms and conditions: (1) This contract to be for a period of three years from the date of its execution subject to renewal by mutual consent.

Second—Said Browne agrees that he will only organize Kiwanis clubs in such places as may be previously approved or designated by the president of the party of the first part; said president shall approve or reject any places designated by said Browne within two weeks after their submission by said Browne to said president.

Third—The initiation fee shall be fifteen dollars per member for each club organized which shall be the sole property of said Browne; no increase in said initiation fee shall be made without the mutual consent of the parties, made in writing. It is agreed that Browne shall not collect initiation fees of any members above the number called for by his contract with the local club being installed, and all initiation fees shall be collected from the local club for members secured by him as per his contract with said local club.

Fourth—It is agreed that the expenses of securing members as hereinbefore set out shall be performed by said Browne.

Fifth—It is agreed by said Browne that he will assign to the party of the first part any and all rights he may have to conduct *The Kiwanis Magazine,* on the execution by the party of the first part of a certain option previously taken.

Sixth—It is further agreed in consideration of the faithful performance by said Browne of his obligations herein the party of the first part agrees that it will not employ or engage any other organizer, International or otherwise, during the life of this contract, said party of the second part having the right to employ such deputies as he may from time to time deem advisable or permit the organization of clubs, except as hereinbefore provided without the consent of said Browne.

Seventh—The said Browne hereby agrees to assign to the Kiwanis Club all his right, title and interest in and to all the insignia, emblems and trademarks of every kind and character pertaining to the name and ideas now and heretofore embodied and invested in the word "Kiwanis" or "Kiwanis Club." Said Browne agrees to assign to the Kiwanis Club the sole and exclusive right to the name "Kiwanis" with all its good will appertaining, it being the intent thereof to invest in the Kiwanis Club all the right, title and interest of said Browne in and to the name "Kiwanis."

That contract was destined to stay in force for one year only. When Kiwanians met for their 1919 International convention at Birmingham, Alabama, a few dozen delegates arrived with their dander up. They said little during the opening amenities—the minute of silence in tribute to Kiwanis war dead, the prayer, the courtesies—but soon thereafter they determinedly went to work. They were a "minority group," and this time they were prepared; they had, indeed, the support of the International Board of Trustees. George H. Ross of Toronto, third vice-president of Kiwanis International, was first spokesman.

"We have a new contract with Mr. Allen Browne, subject to your official ratifications," said he, then offered a resolution that it be ratified.

Most had not heard of it. A new contract with Browne? What's wrong with the one signed last year? Does Browne want more money? Or do we? The questions came in a buzzing of interest. Then the contract was read publicly.

It said, in effect, that Kiwanis was buying itself! The price was to be $17,500, payable to Allen Browne.

The International organization had little money. Where was the $17,500 to come from? Under terms of the contract it was to be paid Browne within twenty-four hours!

Thus another bomb shell burst in another Kiwanis convention, and with only slight imagination we can envision the effects of it. Men leaped to their feet. Others raised hands. All wanted to be heard, and the chairman whammed down so hard and so often with his gavel that the whole rostrum trembled. Here was that "Browne matter" to disrupt things again, when they had hoped for an end to it last year! But here was a wholly new slant.

It was not too surprising, then, that the delegates raised that $17,500 in about an hour. The Baltimore club started with a $500 subscription. Bonds, checks and cash showered down. Men liked the thought of owning their International organization completely! They felt that the organization which Browne founded had snowballed beyond his control—which it most surely had.

He was not the first pioneer to experience such a thing. Indeed, many a person has conceived an idea, nursed it, guided it, and seen it run away from him, perhaps to achieve undying greatness. And in the strange quirks of fate the man himself too often fades into obscurity. Whatever became of Allen Browne, for instance? At the convention a year later, Kiwanians were already asking that. By 1940 not one Kiwanian in a thousand — asked about Allen

Browne — could give more than a blank stare for answer.

The fact is, Allen Simpson Browne, founder of Kiwanis, was never a Kiwanian after his contract was purchased. He died in Dallas, Texas on Sunday, March 18, 1934, in his fifty-first year, and a wife and family survived him. He was a native of Detroit, a graduate of the Detroit public schools, of the University of Michigan and of the Detroit College of Law. But with his restless energy and the vision of a pioneer, he could hardly have settled down to the sedate practice of law. He traveled, he even prospected for mineral wealth, before becoming a professional organizer. George Hixson, first International president, who became Allen's close personal friend and worked intimately with him in Kiwanis, in 1934 said of him:

"We may well regret that we could not have retained the services and counsel of the Kiwanis founder, and that his feelings could not have been spared. But history informs us that no great and enduring movement was ever successfully undertaken, has ever survived, without great pain, sacrifice, and even some injustice. This was no exception."

*   *   *

The trend of Kiwanis thinking-in-the-mass began to show itself more at the 1918 convention than ever before. Three years had passed. Kiwanians had had time to develop some of the attitudes they were destined to carry through the decades. Expression of these attitudes was made by the convention speakers. For one thing, World War I had shocked all people into a reconsideration of life's values, exactly as World War II shocked the present generation. Driven perhaps by fear, and certainly by shame over having permitted a world holocaust, they were ripe for "good" thinking.

The nebulous tendency to make "We Trade" a Kiwanis motto was so thoroughly squelched that its few supporters became negligible. One Kiwanian, a Clevelander, waxed sarcastic about it.

" 'We Trade' what?" he snorted. "You, a dentist, want to trade plates for some of the real estate I sell? That's absurd and you know it. What, then? Do we trade mere pats on the back? Am I to go around town telling everybody what a fine tooth doctor you are, while you go around telling what lovely real estate I peddle? That's even more absurd."

He found virtually unanimous agreement. Bill Marchant of Dayton, Ohio made a rip-snortin' speech at the convention and had the delegates enthralled. "I ask that our organization remember these three U's in dealing with each other and with mankind," he pleaded. "They are Understanding, Unity, and Unselfishness."

If Bill could make the same speech before a mid-century convention, it would surely command the roaring applause given him back there in 1918. For he summed up the whole idealism of Kiwanis. But a summation was not enough. Men of Kiwanis, keyed up emotionally by the war, wanted a more detailed expression of the things they stood for. And fate decreed that a capable man supply it. He was the Reverend J. B. Pengelly, a delegate from Flint,

Michigan. He came before the delegates with a manuscript and was asked to read it aloud. Here it is:

THE KIWANIS WORKING IDEAL

The Kiwanis clubs of the United States and Canada in convention assembled at Providence, Rhode Island in June 1918 present the following statement of their working ideal and desire to make it effective in civic, national and international life.

One of the chief features of our age is the growth of the city. This growth has forced upon us many problems. The members of Kiwanis clubs should teach and practice good fellowship and strive at all times to increase civic unity and usefulness. Every civic enterprise for the development of community welfare should be supported by Kiwanians. Many of our great social problems are not inherently and naturally insoluble but can be solved by able leadership and unselfish service. Every local club should seek every opportunity to build up the inner life of the city through good fellowship and service and thus be big factors in the remaking of our American cities. Our clubs should strive to keep this civic ideal constantly before the people.

The present war is fast creating a new world. The problems of this new world are colossal and tremendously urgent. Every ounce of muscle and nerve, as well as all kinds of wealth and all forms of service, should be consecrated anew to the great work of the United States and their allies in winning this world war for justice and liberty. Every Kiwanis club on this American continent ought to be an active center of patriotism, teaching the people to sacrifice and serve for our holy cause.

In the period following the war new and closer relations will be cemented between the allies. These new relations will offer greater opportunities to the men of this continent. Kiwanians should be urged to study international affairs so as to play a more important part in the new world relations. America, young and vigorous, courageous, keen and wealthy, ought to be inspired and can be inspired to measure up to bigger things.

Our ideal is social. We are interested in our cities, our

nations and our allies. Our ideal is to serve so as to make our cities bigger and better, our nations stronger and victorious and the allies the dominant powers of the world for liberty, justice, progress and happiness. The immortal words of the Great Teacher ought to be our motto: "Let him who is the greatest among you be the servant of all."

When the pastor concluded, absolute silence reigned. It was almost a sacred moment, mind you; people had that exalted, almost tearful look on their faces; inspiration was so thick you could cut it with a knife. Then came one of those impulsive comments likely to crack just such a moment in any meeting. A bull-voiced delegate said—

"That's d - - - good!"

He hadn't meant to be funny. But the crowd exploded in laughter, breaking the emotional tension. The Reverend Pengelly's piece *was* good, and these men knew it. It was a professional expression of the thinking in their own hearts.

*   *   *

Some distinguished thinker has told us that the political reformer and the social reformer must have the time sense of a geologist. Kiwanis leaders, in the early years, were social reformers without knowing it. Some were impatient, truly. They thought that our International conventions paid too much attention to ceremony and courtesy and form, and accomplished too little actual business. Truth is, these impatient ones could not see the ground swell. They were not attuned to the public service that Kiwanis already had rendered, nor to its importance on the American and Canadian scene. Others, more patient, more persistent, helped the new organization through its growing pains, stayed beside it when it might have died, held on to a faith in its goodness. Most of them are unnamed now, unsung, but a few have been honored. One such was Roe Fulkerson.

At a meeting of International officers and trustees on January 23, 1920, Roe Fulkerson, trustee, made a motion that carried unanimously, thereby rounding out the concise and inspired idealism of Kiwanis. It has not been necessary to make any important additions or changes to "the things Kiwanis stands for" even down to mid-century. On that 1920 date, Roe moved for the adoption of the Kiwanis motto. In the March 1920 issue of *The Kiwanis Magazine,* Roe published a brilliant article which explains it. He said:

Over and over again the question has been asked, "What Does Kiwanis Mean?"

If we take the history of the organization and the adoption of the word we find that "Kiwanis" has no meaning, as it was made up of fragments of two or three words. It is a coined word selected for its euphony and at the time of its selection had no more meaning than any other agreeable sounding syllables assembled because they came trippingly off the tongue.

But "Kiwanis" has come to mean something in the world. The idea back of the word has come to loom large for the advancement of civilization on this continent.

Kiwanis sprang into its real being, found itself, coincident with the great world war.

In all the great drives for war loans, for funds to back war charities, and to help the soldiers, Kiwanis built both in the United States and Canada for patriotism, for love of flag and built for the love of the country that flag stood for.

In all our district conventions and through our district organizations Kiwanis has built for love of state or province and has built for the love of all the best traditions of the loyalty in which these district conventions function.

In every city which has a Kiwanis club, that club has built steadily for civic pride. In its work for recreation grounds, for pure politics, for better housing and living conditions, for safety first movements and for every charitable institution of which the city boasts, Kiwanis has made the cities in which it exists better cities to live in. Building for civic betterment has been the big outstanding feature of the movement everywhere.

Kiwanis has everywhere built for better business standards. It is building daily in the minds of businessmen that a competitor is a man to be learned from, rather than a man to be hated, to cooperate with rather than to quarrel with and its business ethics work has built for a better standard among business and professional men everywhere.

So, too, has Kiwanis built up the personality of every man who is one of its members. It has taught him that he need not be tied to the leg of his desk; that it pays in actual cash to come out of his shell and mix with other men, receiving the hearty handclasp that goes with the man who calls him by his first name and eliminates the objectionable "Mister."

So in their wisdom your International officers, assembled recently in Chicago, have adopted "We Build" as the motto of our beloved organization to distinguish its members from the restless horde who in these times of reconstruction are iconoclastic in their tendencies, striving to pull down and destroy the existing order of things.

We Build in Kiwanis.

Twenty-five thousand men welded into one band with one single purpose today—tomorrow fifty thousand and another day a hundred thousand means an influence for good in the world which can and will build a sentiment in favor of the Kiwanis idea which will permeate every cranny and corner of our civilization and be big work, good work, God's work.

YES, WE BUILD.

By 1949 Roe had written millions of words for Kiwanis, and was still writing. But in due course

[51]

his call came; and in due time Roe's many words—which served beautifully in the passing pageantry of our life—will be forgotten, and rightfully so. Yet two words which he left for his fellow men, two inspired words, have already lasted three decades and will serve many more.

Few mortals, indeed, have uttered two words *worth* remembering over the years.

CHAPTER SIX

DISTRICTS ARE BORN

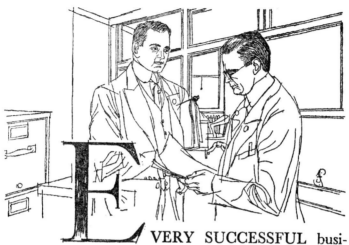

VERY SUCCESSFUL business or professional man has a secret feeling—and sometimes he doesn't keep it secret!—that he could run his club, his town, his state, or indeed his nation, better than the man currently running it.

That masculine conceit is all to the good. In truth, it is not conceit, it is a higher something, more akin to self confidence. It is the something in us which makes us plunge in where angels fear to go. It is the motivating force of the United States and Canada, where Kiwanis has taken deep root. It is, ultimately, the inner force of Kiwanis. It manifests itself in competition for the club presidency down in Harlingen, Texas, and up in Yarmouth, Nova Scotia. It builds a healthy rivalry for club offices in Anchorage, Honolulu, Daytona Beach and Billings. It causes countless huddles in private homes, on lawns, in church basements, in downtown offices, wherever men can get together in reasonable privacy.

The masculine ego, the proclivities toward self assertion, were never more apparent than in those formative years of Kiwanis. It probably took as many spoken words to organize Kiwanis International as it did to organize the first American Congress in 1776. Men accustomed to bossing stood up and tried to boss other men accustomed to bossing. Everybody had ideas to toss in. Altogether it would have confused any outsider trying to take an objective view; certainly it would have confused any citizen of a dictatorship, accustomed to having all his thinking done for him. But in reality, our men were simply "thinking out loud." That's what talk is, in America and Canada in our time. It's our way of airing emotions, cleansing them, opening the way for fellowship and cooperation.

After the convention at Providence in 1918, Kiwanis employed its first full-time paid International secretary, O. Samuel Cummings, to succeed Albert Dodge of Buffalo, New York, who had served without pay as a volunteer officer. He was a big man, mentally and morally—big enough to rise in due time to the positions of International trustee and ultimately to International president. But in 1918 he personified Kiwanis. In him all the endless talk of "we ought to do this" and "we ought to do that" began to crystallize.

It was under Secretary Sam's guidance that Kiwanis performance began to achieve some semblance of uniformity. Theretofore, a club in New York State could and would do pretty much as it pleased, with no thought of its possible effect on a club in Indiana or Oregon. If Kiwanis was to mean much to its own members and to the public at large, it would have to develop some uniform high objectives and ideals. Secretary Sam began stressing that, with excellent results. He also began spreading the arm of Kiwanis. With Allen Browne out of the picture, Sam Cummings had the job of getting new clubs established. It was easier than you might have guessed. Sam had to work hard, yet admittedly got results faster than he anticipated.

"Eighty-three isolated clubs composed Kiwanis when I took office," said he at the Portland convention in 1920. "Now, two years later, we have 267 clubs."

But the numerical growth, 28,541 members at that moment, was dominated by the steadying influence that Sam had brought to his important assignment. He and his co-workers organized not just the facts and figures, not just the physical assets, but the *thinking* of those 28,541 members. It was directional work that only a far-sighted man could have done.

During Sam's administration as International secretary, Kiwanis got its first set of standard club by-laws. Each club was urged also to have the same standing committees. This would enable the organization to move with singleness of purpose. The plan and requirements for membership were tightened down to uniformity. An adequate record system for local club secretaries was established, and a standard operational plan for districts was developed. All of this required the secretary to travel extensively, indeed, to devote virtually every waking hour to Kiwanis welfare. He was paid for it, but he was not paid enough; no servant, who is conscientious in such a position, ever is. In his "spare time" he developed the first efficiently organized International headquarters for Kiwanis. When he felt that it was adequate for handling the organization, it had all of sixteen employees.

"I never dreamed," said George Hixson, the first Kiwanis president, "that headquarters would grow so big."

But then George hardly dared to hope that Kiwanis would reach 25,000 and more members. When membership approximated 250,000 both he and O. Sam Cummings were awed. Today, they beam with pride as they walk through the General Office in Chicago where more than 100 employees are now required to care for essential services.

*   *   *

General Office facilities have grown apace of membership over the decades. The members wanted a central clearing house for friendly counsel and guidance, for exchange of ideas and ideals. The average Kiwanian takes a direct proprietary interest in his home office. Back in his mind, he is always going to pay a visit and see if they are running things properly. An increasing number of them do come in, and from O. Sam Cummings' day the welcome mat has been out. Some can spend only ten minutes. Others stay longer. From them all, the incumbent secretary and his assistants get priceless suggestions, for Kiwanians in the mass constitute a reservoir of information and ideas. Some 1930 letters a day also come into the General Office, and they, too, carry valuable and helpful recommendations.

The ideas and hopes actually gathered from the mass membership, therefore, have become the pattern for Kiwanis performance. This has been reduced to writing so that it can be shared with every club and every individual member. Of necessity, the material had to be condensed, distilled and crystallized into usable form.

Originally, the organization leaders felt that *The Kiwanis Magazine* (including its various early titles) could serve as the clearing house and distribution medium. But as Kiwanis grew, the magazine grew in scope. Today it is more nearly a "general" magazine, guiding Kiwanis in the broader concepts of citizenship and service. This was on demand of the members themselves.

As a result, it was necessary to develop printed suggestions for members and committees. At first they were simply mimeographed. Then small and sometimes not too attractive leaflets began to be used. But as activities increased, as the concept of Kiwanis broadened, all the talent necessary to produce high class "literature" was procured. Staff men and women, carefully trained, in constant contact with the membership by extensive traveling and by mail, write much of the material that is used today. In printing and general eye appeal they are tops. But in context they get down to practical cases; they offer action programs long tested in the American and Canadian fields.

Precisely *how* shall you, a committee chairman, lead your Kiwanis committee in serving agriculture?

An information kit, tabulated, illustrated, wasting no words but lacking no essential detail, is yours for the asking. Precisely *how* shall you function if appointed on the attendance and membership committee of your club, the committee on support of churches in their spiritual aims, or whatever? The answers are available in concise form, worked out over the years from the best experience of thousands of other Kiwanians. Just "write in" for the help you need.

Most of the printed matter from the General Office is beamed at Kiwanians themselves; designed to help them develop strong individual clubs and maintain the best possible programs of service to humanity. But some of the printing is for Kiwanians to pass on to the general public. In this category was the spectacular series of monthly public affairs folders, entitled "It's Fun To Live In America," and its Canadian counterpart, "It's Great To Be A Canadian." Over-all purpose of the series was to remind Americans and Canadians that the system of individual enterprise is without equal, hence a direct challenge to communist ideology. The pamphlets apparently struck the right note with Kiwanians and other American leaders, in view of the fact that 16,-250,000 copies were distributed in one year.

*   *   *

Actual mechanics of the International organization began to be a concern of Kiwanians even before O. Sam Cummings became its first full-time secretary. Prior to 1918 much talk was heard about a "federation" of Kiwanis clubs, yet nobody seemed to know exactly what was meant by federation. But in that year, Kiwanians in Michigan and in New England began to talk about organizing into districts. No one mapped a concrete plan for it until the convention at Providence in June. A committee, appointed to introduce a new Constitution, brought forth a district plan which, with occasional variations and improvements, is used to this day. Subsequently, the exact purpose of the district was stated concisely. It is not legislative, but educational, promotional, cooperative. Here is the official wording:

"To seek within the district and through the clubs of the district the attainment of the Objects of Kiwanis International as set forth in the Constitution.

"To cooperate with Kiwanis International in building new clubs and in educating and strengthening clubs within the district.

"To promote participation of the clubs in the district in the general objectives, programs and policies of the district and of Kiwanis International."

From the individual districts stems much of the chronological and political history of Kiwanis. The format established in 1918 has created an *esprit de corps* among clubs which enables each to operate according to its local opportunities and needs and yet feel a close part of the powerful International organization. It has worked out precisely that way, and today the district plan is held to be eminently successful. Kiwanians take a special pride in district affairs, as well as in club and International activities. Notable recent instances are in the Wisconsin-Upper Michigan and Texas-Oklahoma Districts.

"Through development of our industry," a leader in Wisconsin reported, "many of our 10,000 lakes and our streams were becoming polluted by the wastes from paper mills and other factories. These natural waters are our most valuable assets. Some drastic conservation measure had to be taken."

Two big agencies had already tried unsuccessfully to end that pollution, one being the state government itself. Existing laws against pollution could not be enforced because enforcement would cripple the economy of the entire area. So district Kiwanis leaders sought a long-range program of correction.

First move was to gather accurate information as to the extent of the pollution. Virtually every club in the district cooperated in the survey. The Kiwanis leaders then contacted government research bureaus in the hope of finding a way to make something useful from those factory wastes rather than just dumping them, or, failing that, to find a safe method of disposal. This entire effort may take five years or longer, but the Kiwanians are prepared to see it through.

In addition, Kiwanians in that district voluntarily took on two other major public service efforts. One was the planting of living snow fences. Snow control is an annual problem there and a costly one. The other was extensive reforestation. Again this required detailed preliminary study and much field work, not simply by an appointed committee but by almost every Kiwanian in the district. All of these district-wide service projects were accepted in addition to routine work for underprivileged children and comparable club services long established.

CHAPTER SEVEN

A WRITING FELLOW GETS A HORNET

IT IS RATHER imperative
that any organization of one hundred or more members have some printed medium for supplying information of common interest and importance. Thus we have that typically American institution, the house organ, and by extension, the fraternal magazine. A few such are distinguished.

One of them first appeared in February 1917, at Cleveland. It held to a standard cover design—an Indian before his wigwam, engaged in peaceful trading with paleface trappers. Title of the journal was *The Kiwanis Club*. Best that can be said about it is that it was mediocre in quality and general reader interest. Its owner and editor had so doggoned much else to do that he couldn't devote time to his journal. He was the same Allen Simpson Browne who also owned Kiwanis. He himself knew the journal's shortcomings, but he had hopes of making it good.

He quickly learned, among other things, that it was infeasible to ship the journal in bundles to various club secretaries and expect them to distribute a copy to each member. Somehow that system never worked. But enough copies did get around so that Kiwanians were aware of its potentialities. A few were critical of it.

"Its cover slogan says, 'Cooperation and Reciprocation'," one member jibed. "How does that translate?"

That was truly a rotundly oratorical phrase meaning very little unless broken down to personal application. It was typical of its era, however, and typical of the magazine's weaknesses. Nevertheless, the journal as a whole had merit enough to make Kiwanians recognize the possibilities for a better and permanent one. By the time of the International convention at Providence in 1918, they were ready to take action.

"Our magazine must be controlled by the club at large," said delegate B. G. Watson of Columbus, Ohio. "It must be a journal of high standard. It must be professionally edited, and must not be political, personal, narrow or sectional."

His fellow delegates promptly endorsed his stand and bought the existing magazine from its founder, Allen Browne. They then scanned the Kiwanis horizons for a new editor.

Among those present was the president of the Washington, D. C. club, a "writing fellow" who had already shown a kindly sense of humor and an intuitive good taste. The International trustees called him into a huddle with them. He knew most of the answers about magazine production and was glad to give them. Then human nature took its normal course.

"Look," said one trustee, "Roe knows everything we don't, he's thoroughly familiar with magazines. I move we make him editor."

Many another authority, talking freely about a Kiwanis committee's work, has suddenly awakened to find himself chairman of said committee! It was so with that gentleman from Washington, a man destined to serve Kiwanis with distinction until 1949, Roe Fulkerson. Stuck with the assignment by genial friends, Roe could only swallow hard and mumble, "I'll do the best I can." Editing a magazine for Kiwanis was the last thing he had dreamed of doing. Here is his own report of how he went to work:

I was told I was editor, so I went back to Washington and produced the first number, describing a convention of which there was no printed program and of which I had made no notes. I had no mailing list, either, because previously the publication had been distributed hand to hand. I wrote the first edition from cover to cover as I also did for the next two years. I had no notes and no mailing list, and soon I discovered that I had no money to pay printers. During the two years before subscription money began to come in, I financed the magazine myself, having loaned the book four thousand dollars before a cent came back. But *The Kiwanis Hornet* went to press and came out regularly, as did its successors.

The Kiwanis Hornet confessed to being the official publication of the Kiwanis clubs of the United States and Canada. It further described itself as "A Periodical of Personality and Pep." Don't sneer, even genially, at such a slogan. That was the era when the great American magazine was making a big thing out of personality articles. The word "pep" was alive and vibrant in American slang. Roe Fulkerson and his *Kiwanis Hornet* were thoroughly abreast of the times. Format was about like that of the present *Reader's Digest,* which was then being conceived by an ambitious chap recovering from a war wound, Dewitt Wallace.

Yet there were certain requirements for a "house organ"—a journal for a specific organization—which the *Hornet* was not fulfilling. Roe was no rut rider. He kept in contact with the International officers. He and they kept alert to reader responses; if Kiwanians had anything to say about the magazine, they listened. As a result, the name *Hornet* was dropped after two issues, and *The Kiwanis Torch* appeared. It called itself "A Periodical of Personality," dropping the slangy "pep" as being a bit undignified, which it was for men outstanding in business and professional life. Size of the magazine was changed to seven and one-half by ten and one-half inches. Roe himself seemed to gather more and more enthusiasm, which was reflected in the increasingly inspirational editorial content.

In 1920 the name of the journal was changed once more. *Torch* smacked just a little of high-schoolishness men were saying. And Kiwanis was not a youth organization. Other men, discussing the matter, asked why we must have any sort of symbolic title. Why *Hornet* or *Torch* or any such? Upshot was a decision to make it simply *The Kiwanis Magazine.* Its first issue, March 1920, also showed on the cover the motto, "We Build" — first publication of the present Kiwanis motto. Of that issue, 25,000 copies were printed. The official magazine, as with the organization itself, had grown to powerful proportions in just three years.

*　*　*

Appearance and styling have been changed—as they should be, constantly, forever, in the interest of progress. By constitutional provision in 1921, the International secretary became the editor-in-chief of the journal. A managing editor and staff of experts work with him — in the art, photography, layout, advertising departments — all the branches of this highly specialized profession.

The Kiwanis Magazine is not published for profit. In fact, no phase of Kiwanis International is designed for organization profit. The high idealism of the club requires sacrifice; a *giving* rather than a getting. Yet, in the long run, it is inevitably true that he who gives most gets most.

*　*　*

Content of the magazine in recent years, especially since the end of World War II, has been comparable to the more serious aspects of *The Saturday Evening Post, Nation's Business, Christian Century,* and such commercial journals of interest to men of high intelligence. No fiction (with rare exceptions) is carried. The articles are not "highbrow" in the sense that only an Oxford scholar can wade through them. But they are penetrating. They are short. They are rich with precedent for community, national and personal improvement and are implemented with more than average "how-to."

[65]

Readers of the magazine include doctors, lawyers, newspaper men, educators, clergymen, merchants, industrialists and a thousand other business and professional classifications.

The Kiwanis Magazine is written for some 275,000 men comprising every type of honest male leadership in the United States and Canada. In the main, they are well-to-do financially, blessed with a community consciousness and a know-how to get things done.

Much of the magazine's undertone is spiritual. Not sectarian, not denominational, but spiritual. God as a reality is likely to appear in its columns by implication and by name. Kiwanians, the editors have learned, are not averse to talking about God; indeed, virtually every Kiwanis meeting is opened with prayer.

But alongside an inspirational article is likely to be one of down-to-earth grappling with facts. For instance, "The Plague of Urban Clamor" in one issue lays out the bare truth of city noises, reports their tremendous toll in health and happiness, and shows how to abate them. Reasonable space is allocated in each issue to news of what Kiwanis clubs are doing, what services they are rendering, especially when these could be a precedent for action elsewhere.

Such, then, is the pattern for the modern magazine that grew out of the original house organ started in 1917.

It is heartening to remember that Roe Fulkerson wrote continuously for the magazine until his death on January 11, 1949. It is doubtful if any other individual and magazine ever were more closely integrated than these two. Old time Kiwanians say

that Roe *was* the magazine. He became Kiwanis'
official scribe — a marble pedestal, supporting a
bronze bust of him, at the General Office proclaims
that fact for posterity.

CHAPTER EIGHT

"WHAT'S GOOD FOR DAD IS GOOD FOR ME"

OMETIME IN the not too distant future — so a legend goes — the *men* of America will have offended God so relentlessly that He will be compelled to eliminate them from the face of the earth. It may be because they have permitted war. It may be because they have neglected to place a proper value on the home, church and school, or because they have allowed hunger and disease to run rampant in certain sections of the world—oh, there is ample cause!

If and when He does smite us, though, it will not be the end of mankind. For He is a compassionate God, and will keep our seed alive and growing. He will—says the legend—simply turn our world over to our up-and-coming sons.

It may be that Kiwanians have sensed the warning in that legend. For in the rapid rise of Kiwanis they have allowed—and then encouraged—their sons to rise in a comparable organization through America's high schools.

Key Club International here in mid-century has become significant in both size and service record.

Key Clubs are service clubs scaled down to high school ages and high school activities. Their motto also is "We Build," and it is not a casual mouthing, but is a direct orientation of youth. They are not—let this be known officially and with emphasis—a training ground for Kiwanis membership later; no Key Clubber can automatically matriculate into Kiwanis. If and when he becomes an adult and earns a place of importance in some business or profession, and if his moral integrity is known, and if he aspires to be a leader among men serving humanity, then he may indeed become a member of some service organization. Key Clubbers are junior Kiwanians only in sponsorship and similarity of ideals.

The Key Club development was not a deliberate planning. That is, the men of Kiwanis did not consciously set out to organize their sons. But in Sacramento, the capital of California, in the spring of 1925, high school administrators sat in a huddle one day.

"Graduation time is nearing," said one. "And while we have taught our youngsters many things, we haven't given them a proper vocational guidance."

"Right," another man agreed. "But we lack the training for that. Could we bring in some community leaders for it? Could we—I'm just thinking out loud — organize the school boys, the serious-minded ones, who want to plan their careers intelligently, and help them find proper guidance?"

It was a thought to mull over. And as matters stood, those two men were not only teachers, they were Kiwanians. Other executives in the school system were Kiwanians, too, and so inevitably the thinking turned toward their club. Kiwanis had a strong youth program, they knew. What better place to turn?

Upshot of it all was that in May of that year, 1925, Sacramento High School organized the first Key Club in history. A quarter-century later it was still going strong. It held to its original purpose, vocational guidance, but immediately expanded to become a complete service organization for the whole school in much the manner that a Kiwanis club serves the whole community. No hard and fast set of service activities was adopted, but the program was made flexible so that any need could be met as it arose.

Fifteen years had to pass before Key Clubs as an organization really amounted to much. During that interval they expanded "by word of mouth" only. Some traveler happened into Sacramento, chanced to learn about Key Club there, and started one in his home town. Or some club in another city heard about Sacramento's success, wrote for advice, then started one. In every case the boys loved it. Key Club, it was found, offered the youths the essentials of a fraternity but without the undemocratic exclusiveness and with more than mere social interest. The Key Club had the essence of idealism. The boys had the energies to implement it.

Key Club, which was founded in the far West, jumped over most of the continent during that fifteen years and took deep root in the East, especially in Florida, Kentucky, Louisiana, Pennsylvania and New Jersey. By 1939 there were seventy-five Key Clubs, mostly in those states. And in that year, the first plan was begun for combining the clubs into federated groups. With Kiwanis counsel, a convention was scheduled and held at Fort Lauderdale, Florida, and an Association of Key Clubs of Florida was formed.

"We simply saw that California had a good thing," one Florida Kiwanian jibed, "and so we reached out to take it and improve it."

"Every good thing originates in California," the westerner shot back, with perhaps a modicum of truth.

Their good-natured rivalry about it, plus other talk about the Key Clubs then being heard wherever Kiwanians met, served to stimulate interest in the whole movement. Wherefore, by 1944 delegates from Louisiana, Mississippi, Tennessee and Florida met in the very first "International" Key Club convention at Gainesville, Florida. A curly-haired chap, handsome enough to thrill any high school girl, and poised enough to delight any mother or father, was elected first "International" president. He was Malcolm Lewis of West Palm Beach, Florida. Next year, in the convention at Lakeland, Florida, Edward Richardson of Fort Lauderdale became president, and he too had the charm that only an outstanding high school boy can show. These two worked prodigiously at their jobs. During their administrations a strong

Constitution and bylaws were developed, polished and made ready for adoption at the third convention. This was held at New Orleans on April 27, 1946.

Kiwanis as the parent organization was benevolently aloof—after the manner of parents—toward Key Clubs for several years. The International Board of Trustees officially recognized Key Club success in 1942. That year the board "recommended" Key Clubs to all Kiwanis clubs.

In 1944, the board created a special Kiwanis International Committee on Sponsored Youth Organizations, with the primary duty of looking after Key Club expansion. Forthwith Key Clubs began to expand, even in the harassment of war. When the victory had been won, Key Clubbers were harder than ever to push around; youth had literally saved America's and Canada's life, boys still young in years had taken gigantic fortresses and beaten the attackers into submission. In the spring of 1946, a fully staffed Key Club Department was put into operation. At that time there were 112 Key Clubs in operation, with 2464 boys. By early 1962 the movement had grown to 2205 clubs with 54,548 members. Thus, in both number and prestige Key Clubs had become one of the greatest organizations for high school boys ever developed.

*   *   *

It is a fact, therefore, that many an eager lad has plumped into his home one day and said, "Mom! Dad! Can I join the Key Club? I mean, may I?"

Doubtless it is a fact, too, that Mom and Dad have hedged. They are accustomed to Junior's sudden enthusiasm. They have learned (by high school time) not to be caught off guard.

"What's it all about, dear?" Mom has demanded. And, "What will it cost?" Pop has chimed in.

Junior of course had the answers — he always does! What *is* it all about? Mom's interest was logical. Junior had only to hand her a little booklet —*Constitution and Bylaws, Key Club International* —and point to Page 1, Article II. It says:

"The objects of Key Club International shall be:
   "To develop initiative and leadership.
   "To provide experience in living and working together.
   "To serve the school through its administrative officers and the community.
   "To prepare for useful citizenship."

How well the boys have lived up to those objectives is a matter for perusal and pride. Much of their work is trivial by adult standards — polishing the school trophy case, furnishing mirrors for the school rest rooms, serving meals at a charity dinner, laying a brick wall between Science Hall and Auditorium. But in the aggregate it's the little services in life that build up the big ones; Key Clubbers seldom bite off more than they can chew. But most of the projects undertaken are not small. Many cost the boys long hours of labor, much pocket money and much sacrifice of time and convenience. Every club has been required to make an annual report of activities to the General Office. Those reports, even when modestly phrased, are long and inspiring.

"But the best thing about those clubs," one Kiwanis officer said, "is the attitude they build in the boys themselves. No adult American or Canadian could help being proud of a typical Key Club lad."

That attitude has now been reflected in many a fine Key Club graduate, young men who have faced life poised and self-assured, humble yet confident. Some have achieved distinction. One is Ralph Edwards, who rose to the very top among America's great radio and television artists, and who also became known as a man devoted to humanitarian service. He was an active Key Clubber in the Oakland, California, High School. The other was Alexander R. "Sandy" Nininger, Jr., a scholarly West Pointer who for heroic fighting in hand-to-hand combat on Bataan, became the first soldier to receive the Congressional Medal of Honor in World War II, and who then gave his life in battle that the rest of us might continue to live. He was a charter member of the Key Club in Ft. Lauderdale, Florida, High School. Thus the two states that did most to "pioneer" Key Clubs are honored with two Key Clubbers whom younger generations can hold in high respect and admiration.

*   *   *

But all boys are not grown, you will say, when they leave high school. Does Kiwanis interest in youth end at graduation time?

Kiwanis leaders recently have seen in this a field for significant expansion of service. Nevertheless there are certain problems which attend any organization of the graduates and bigger boys, the college ages, into service clubs. It is a moment when birds fly the nest, when boys "leave home." On their own, they scatter, in physical fact and in mental diversion.

They begin that inevitable straining for a toe hold into the world of adults, and of necessity most of this is competitive, hence in self defense. This is not necessarily "wrong," but it consumes energies and time. Boys in college and college-age boys out of college need a few years to level off.

With those psychological factors in mind, Kiwanis has offered opportunities for college boys in Circle "K" International. The first Circle K Club was founded at Washington State College, Pullman, Washington, in 1936 by Jay N. Emerson who ten years later became President of Kiwanis International. This club, known as Circle K Fraternity, was sponsored by the Kiwanis Club of Pullman.

The Circle K fraternity idea was geared to the local needs of Washington State. The idea did not spread as such. In 1947 the first Circle K Club as a service organization for the college man was organized by the Kiwanis Club of Carthage, Illinois, at Carthage College. Subsequent growth was rapid. However, Circle K Clubs were operated as local projects of individual Kiwanis clubs in college towns until 1955. That year Kiwanis International officially recognized Circle K International and set up a Circle K Department at the General Office to work with this newest sponsored youth organization. By early 1962 the movement had grown to 362 clubs with 7,257 members.

Circle K as with Key Clubs and Kiwanis Clubs gives primacy to deeper spiritual considerations rather than to materialistic thinking, and its service programs are therefore of the highest possible order.

CHAPTER NINE

"A MARTIN ASKINS CAME ALONG"

AMONG THE hackneyed and partially truthful statements which you can hear concerning the service clubs in America is this: "Rotarians own the town, Kiwanians run the town, and Lions enjoy the town."

Kiwanis is pleased herewith to plead guilty to its part of the charge! Down the years Kiwanis' history has grown richer and richer with records of "running" important public services in communities of the United States and Canada. This is not to be invidious—there is no serious competition, no lack of cordiality among the great service organizations; and by the very nature of their ideals, never can be. But the history of Kiwanis service is inspiring. A truly active "running," a vitalized personal giving by individual Kiwanians of time, talent and money, has become a primary function of the organization. It is not a thing for light or casual interest; it is almost a sacred thing.

The service program of Kiwanis began to reach maturity before the organization was five years old. By 1930 it had become farflung indeed. Today it is beyond the conception of any one mind. It is among the few truly magnificent developments in the life of man on this continent. Statistics about it are staggering, yet these do not begin to show the greatness of it, because the individual club officers can gather and report only such service efforts as are "official" in the club program, and because the individual Kiwanian does incredible work quietly on his own.

As the urge to render that unselfish service became apparent, the need for organization and direction of it became apparent, too. That's when the International headquarters came into being. Relatively few Kiwanians, even today, realize that the General Office in Chicago exists primarily to implement and integrate the now vast service program of the clubs throughout two nations. All the physical plant, all the accounting, bookkeeping, personnel direction, literally everything at the home office, has been gradually developed to make Kiwanis a *service* rather than a luncheon club. The command to do this came from the Kiwanians themselves. They wanted no other kind of organization.

Over the years, then, a breakdown of service fields has been effected, and constant, direct and personal club aids flow from the General Office. In the beginning years a Kiwanian might have had the urge but not the know-how for public service. Today he has the most skilled guidance that experts can devise. It is based on need and on long experience. As of this writing, fifteen major divisions of service—sixteen action programs—emanate from Kiwanis International. These are Agriculture and Conservation, Public and Business Affairs for Canada and the United States, Support of Churches in Their Spiritual Aims, Boys and Girls Work, Key Clubs, Circle K, Underprivileged Child, Achievement Reports, Attendance and Membership, Inter-Club Relations, Kiwanis Education and Fellowship, New Club Building, Programs and Music, Public Relations, and Vocational Guidance. Part of it, of necessity, deals with Kiwanis administration—maintaining the vehicle for cooperative effort and individual inspiration. But far and away the greatest emphasis is placed on Citizenship Service and Youth Service, because through the years Kiwanians have indicated that in such realms is where the major heart interest lies.

While the vastness of the program is such that no adequate recording of it is possible, any written history would be valueless without representative exhibits; without several specific samples of what kind of service Kiwanis has been rendering. It has proved true also that the Number One love seems to be for service to underprivileged children—the physically or mentally handicapped, the delinquent, the needy in any form. This is understandable. It is the expression of the Kiwanian of his love for the family, that unit of society on which civilization itself is built. If *any* child thus is denied some of the privileges, he is instantly willing to shuck off his coat and work to correct it. Let us look at some of the things he has done.

*   *   *

Exactly at ten o'clock in the morning on New Year's Day, 1949, a magnificent parade swung down the main street of a medium-sized American city. It had thirty-six floats, thirty-six bands, all the beauty and splendor that could be imagined. More than 200,000 spectators lined the curbs, cheering. The parade ended at a stadium where at 1:30 one of the renowned "Bowl" games was played to a capacity crowd. The parade had brought many thousands of dollars into the economy of the town, through people who came to march in it or see it, and net proceeds from the game totaled several thousand more—all of which went into a fund to aid handicapped children.

Heading that parade, just behind the colors, a youngish middle-aged man rode alone in the back seat of a convertible. He was so self-conscious because of his prominence there that he lost his usual affable smile and just stared straight ahead. A small sign on his car said, "Parade Chairman." Ninety per cent of the spectators never knew his name— nor does it matter to us here. For the sake of discussion let's give him an average Kiwanis name— Martin Askins.

Marty, a little investigation would reveal, has been a Kiwanian for about twenty-five years. He is president of a leading mercantile establishment in his town, although in 1918, when the Armistice was signed, he was flat on his back in a war hospital and hadn't a dime to his name. He is of average build, has a touch of baldness, dresses informally but not flashily. He has a clear, concise speaking voice, but makes a few mistakes in grammar and is not immune to telling old jokes. He has a perfect record of Kiwanis attendance—once he chartered a plane and flew 200 miles to make up a missed meeting, after which the boys all said that his name, "Martin," honoring the bird, was an apt one. He has his first wife and three kids, two of whom have won honors in high school while the third captains his grade school baseball and football teams. He can break ninety at golf, on good days, and he throws his weight around some in gin rummy. He goes to church, is a deacon, in fact. He enjoys the movies, although he sometimes dozes in them.

It was Martin Askins—Marty—who took over when the Kiwanis plans for a parade and Bowl football game seemed hard to jell in June of 1948. The same Kiwanis club tried to stage a Bowl game the year before. Indeed they had staged a game, but a mediocre one, so lacking in showmanship and imagination—and in hard work—that it lost the club nearly $4000.

"I am personally ashamed of us," Marty told his fellow Kiwanians, in the mourning session following that first game. "Here we are, a group of 175 business and professional leaders in our city unable to handle a little sports event that any average promoter from Hollywood could have staged single-handed."

"Second the motion," somebody spoke up.

"Thank you," Marty went on. "And before somebody suggests that we abandon the project, admitting failure, I hereby volunteer to serve on the Bowl game committee for next year. Mr. President, please call on me for any service I can render."

The applause was vigorous and meaningful.

Inevitably, of course, Marty ended up as chairman of the Bowl committee. He had expected it. In June he went to work. He picked a dozen men to help him. They had many meetings, in living rooms, in offices, on lawns. By September they knew exactly what kind of New Years Day festival they would offer. They traveled throughout their state arranging for high school bands and queens and floats. They recruited other Kiwanians to get publicity, to handle the Bowl ticket sales, to police the parade, to be responsible for the endless details of such a festival. *They worked.* Marty Askins gave unreasonably of his own time and talents—but loved every minute of it. He was everywhere at once. He was tireless. He spent his own money. He asked nothing for himself. He ignored the pessimists, strode over the conservatives and moved audaciously ahead.

No wonder, then, the others put Marty at the head of that grand parade. He deserved it, even though it embarrassed him.

He is the perfect embodiment of the perfect Kiwanian.

He is not too numerous, even in Kiwanis, but he is the ideal. He is the man, the type, who implements the whole magnificent Kiwanis program of unselfish service to humanity.

He and his kind are the ones referred to when Kiwanians say "We Build."

* * *

The story of Marty Askins (true to the last detail, except for his name) has been duplicated in spirit and in amount of effort expended almost since the first day of Kiwanis existence. Away back yonder in 1918, for example, one of the Ohio clubs saw a need for $400 to aid a widow with a child who was partially blind.

"Let's think up something in which all the members can take part," one Kiwanian suggested, "and raise some money at the same time. Fellowship and profit."

"Sure!" another agreed. "How about a minstrel show."

That was the era when blackface minstrels were dying, but these men didn't know that. They agreed unanimously to stage such a show — with singers, jugglers, vaudeville skits, comedians, all the traditional things. It would be local talent, but good.

Unfortunately, having endorsed the project, the club men then sat back and twiddled their thumbs. Committees somehow just didn't function. Everybody seemed to wait for everybody else to move first. Finally an auditorium was rented, tickets were printed, announcements made, a few ideas aired, but that vital spark of enthusiasm, which has to appear in every such project, seemed not to ignite.

Then a Martin Askins came along.

He was simply one of the members. He was a popular fellow—he always is. He was successful in his personal business and was an exceedingly "busy" man—he always is. But he began to demonstrate a *direct, individual responsibility* for the success of that minstrel show. Before he realized it, he was chairman of the project—he nearly always is!

It is hardly necessary to tell you how he functioned, and what happened. You have all seen him in action. Just know that in this instance the Kiwanis club raised not $400 but $1123.70 net for aiding the widow and any other unfortunates. And they had a whopping good time doing it.

Intimate study of Kiwanis records for these forty-odd years shows that every club in every state and province is loaded with "knife and fork" members. The term "knife and fork" often is used in contempt. It shouldn't be. For it does not follow that the Kiwanian who just comes to meetings, eats and sits, for several weeks at a stretch, is without value. Truth is, he can and does suddenly become the workhorse of the organization when need arises. Not all of us can be Marty Askinses. We are not all endowed with the physical good looks, the engaging personalities, the lucky breaks in life generally, to be generals and admirals in civilian armies. Nevertheless, we too can think.

"I wish to thank Bill—and Ed—especially," declared Martin Askins of that parade enterprise, after the event. "They said little while all the planning was going on, yet on several occasions they put a brake on me and my committees. They were thinking deeply, anticipating trouble that we would surely have encountered. But for them we would have made several serious mistakes."

The Kiwanis records show that men who can head a parade committee or a minstrel show committee or a golf tournament committee cannot function so well at aiding churches in their spiritual aims, or at installing the equipment for a slum district playground. Men have varying emotional structures. Some are, or appear to be, lethargic by nature; they sit back in their chairs, sleepy-eyed, listening to the others talk, apparently taking little or no interest. More than likely they simply have glandular activity different from the peppery gents; they could use some thyroid treatments. But they serve, as Marty indicated, as levelers. They serve much like the comptroller or the auditor does in a big business organization—he who watches the enthusiasm of the noisier bosses and at the right moment reaches out with restraining hand. Success of Kiwanis rests perhaps more than any other one thing on the ability of club officers to recognize those divergent, varying talents among the members.

The degree to which such talents have been recognized is almost unbelievable. Continuous records of Kiwanis club achievements throughout the United States and Canada have been kept until their volume now taxes the space available in the General Offices at Chicago. Historically they are priceless, yet no single volume—no dozen volumes—of printed history could begin to list them. They are a backing of precedent for any doubting Thomas who might appear, or for any younger-generation Kiwanis club that needs a light of guidance. When you pick reports from those files, even at random, you find them absorbing.

One noon in Phoenix, Arizona Kiwanians were awarding gold watches to high school graduates who had shown the most progress toward knowledge and citizenship. A handsome, well-poised lad stood up to receive his, then walked gracefully to the speaker's microphone.

"You gentlemen will not remember me," said he, earnestly, "but I am the same boy whom you held up on this same table fifteen years ago, as one of the club-footed orphans you were helping. My gratitude is beyond words."

He paused for a long, long moment just looking at those Kiwanians, his eyes glistening but with his head erect. He could say no more. He did not need to; did not need to say a routine thank you for his new watch. Finally he turned slowly, went back to his chair and sat down. All that while the huge dining room was held in a dramatic silence. For those men were touched. Touched, as few men ever are. Because it is not often that we are privileged to see the full measure of results that accrue from some unselfish kindness shown.

No less moving, but with a hint of whimsy to lessen the heart pull, is the true story of a service rendered in Philadelphia. A little girl was among those befriended, and so Kiwanians received a letter:

> Dear Sirs I am six and a one-half. I am going to have a serus—oper—oper—[she never quite finished the word operation]. Aunty says you will have to pay for it goody but if i die and go to heaven you can have my wagon and purse the blue one i may not die . . . Love. Alise.

The committee of Kiwanians wisely decided not to make publicity of so fine a letter. But you can bet that "serus operation" was followed with more interest than all the doing in Washington, London, Moscow and Berlin that week. In due time, praise God, Alise could write her thank you note. It came, obviously dictated, expressing gratitude for the club's generosity. But the charming tyke had her own postscript:

I did not die so I will keep the wagon and purse.

* * *

Kiwanians are likely to lend their collective and individual hands to literally anything that needs attention in their home communities. There is a tiny club down in Texas where the town hadn't progressed to the point of having any plumbing for its schools. When Kiwanis was two months old there, news reached the club that the outdoor privies at school were in a deplorable state.

Now, the Kiwanians could have written a check, hiring some handy man of the town to make the necessary repairs. Instead, the club held its next official meeting—of all places!—inside that school privy.

Attendance was ninety-four per cent, at first. A check-up was taken, and adjournment was voted until the missing brethren could be located. One was "tied up in conference" at his office. His club men promptly untied him. Another was at home sick, but not too sick to get up, grinning, and come along. He detoured via his garage and got a long handled shovel, a hammer, nails and a saw.

By four o'clock that afternoon, the school privies were completely sanitary, enclosed, screened, repaired and painted. *Next* week the Kiwanians had the school trustees for luncheon guests. And the next September the kids found water toilets, washrooms, drinking fountains and even shower baths at their school.

*　　*　　*

Thus in aiding handicapped children, Kiwanians over the years have tacitly told the world that "We Build" not for ourselves but for future generations. It is one way of implementing the Christian ideal, is an expression of basic selflessness approved by men of high type religions everywhere. Yet Kiwanians dare not pat themselves on the back because of their goodness. In truth, they are partly selfish about it, having discovered that most priceless secret of all —that only the *un*selfish ever know happiness!

"I'm not such a saint!" roared one Kiwanian, embarrassed when fellow townsmen praised his leadership. "I'm not even very good at handling kids, not patient or tolerant enough. But I get peace of mind out of working for them, and that's more than I get out of money grabbing."

Kiwanis as an institution has set no limits on how needy children shall be helped. It is a matter to be decided by the individual club, then by the individual club member. The United States and Canada have nearly 5,000,000 school children with defective hearing, for instance, and when Kiwanis learned that eighty-five per cent of those defects could be cured, it went into action. If Kiwanis history showed no other record of public service, it would still have justified itself there alone.

One first move was to see that local clinics were organized to examine every child, in an effort to detect the hard-of-hearing ones. This work began several years ago and is still under way. It is a never-ending job, for the clinics must be supported, improved, encouraged constantly. Then treatments and hearing aids must be provided for those children whose parents are not inclined or not able to provide them. *Must* be? Literally that. An acceptance of the "must" in such instances is the difference between democracy and totalitarianism, between civilization and savagery. America as a nation accepted it from the beginning. Kiwanis and kindred service groups have expanded it as a principle, a way of life.

The same clinical aid is given to cripples through the United States and Canada, Alaska, Yukon and Hawaii. No child in genuine need will be turned away by Kiwanis if he were born club-footed, if he is a spastic, if he is twisted or handicapped in any way. Millions of dollars already have been spent in this field by Kiwanians; millions, billions more will be made available, for there is no end to the generosity of high type men. It is true, too, in helping those with defective eyes, defective speech, with nutritional problems and with unfortunate moral influences.

"I had more downright fun," one Kiwanian wrote, "building a fence around a new Kiwanis playground than I did going on a moose hunting trip the month before. We gave every evening for a month to the hammer-and-saw work. We put up basketball posts, laid out baseball diamonds, erected backstops, did the plumbing for a shower room. I helped one little boy unbutton his clothes to strip down for the first shower bath he had ever seen, the first bath of *any* kind he had experienced in years, if I guessed rightly. He was happier than if Santa Claus had called. He bathed four times, drying off each time. When he finally started home, he asked if he could bring his mother over to bathe their baby. We had not planned for that, but we promptly arranged to bathe that whole family. They were just one of some dozen cases, too.

"Three years later the local juvenile judge spoke at a Kiwanis meeting, and said that juvenile delinquency in the district where we had put the new playground had dropped eighty-eight per cent."

That kind of report is not rare. It is routine. It enriches the whole history of Kiwanis, by thousands of instances in cities and towns throughout the two nations. In the aggregate, statistics about it will astonish you, and personalized studies will wring your heart.

Combating delinquency in physique, health and morals has extended to "boys work" in endless forms. In some instances the work becomes much like the dad playing with his son's new electric train—dad re-lives his own youth, perhaps improving it, compensating for early needs in his own life.

That sort of masculine interest extends also to baseball, football, basketball, swimming, all sports and recreations, not to duplicate or conflict with other existing agencies for youth services, but to supplement them. Most of Kiwanis' efforts have been for the underprivileged. Often it can be done through YMCA and YWCA organizations. A typical Kiwanis Craft Shop in the local "Y" has hundreds of boys—who could otherwise have no such wholesome opportunity — working with saws and hammers, leather tools, paint brushes, plastics and such, every day in the week. Kiwanis pays the bills, and annually the sponsoring club inspects the work being done, in a special meeting.

More and more of that subtle ingredient, imagination, is being poured into Kiwanis youth work. Back in 1937 the West Toronto, Ontario club took over an entire castle—Casa Loma, on a hill, complete with turrets, battlements, moat, dungeons, and every storybook thing—and converted it into a tourist attraction. Money proceeds began to swell the fund for aiding handicapped children. That club raised $50,000 in seven years for children's work. It might logically have sat back to rest on its laurels. But report to the members of the $50,000 earned served only to stimulate greater effort. That's the Canadian way and the American way. It is a way, moreover, that many lesser nations have never understood.

* * *

Not all Kiwanis children's work is for the "needy." Often a service is rendered to the healthy, well-to-do children of Kiwanians themselves—this through an increasingly popular field of endeavor known as vocational guidance.

It became apparent some thirty years ago that many youths, indeed most of them, went into business life more or less haphazardly.

"I want to be an engineer," said one, "because they get to build bridges."

But gentle guidance showed him to be totally disinterested in the mathematics and mechanics of any engineering. And in the end he became an actor of distinction, then a radio star.

Kiwanians, working intimately with school superintendents, principals and teachers (many of whom were themselves in Kiwanis clubs), began tightening down the science of choosing a career. Records now show that hundreds of thousands of young men and women have been helped toward happy careers. "I had thought I wanted to be a model," one girl wrote her Kiwanis patrons. "At least I said I did. Secretly I wanted to get married and be a mother in a happy home. Your speaker came to our school and showed us how that could be the noblest career of all. And it *is* too! I have exactly what I wanted. My husband is doing fine. As soon as he gets a little older, and we get our two babies (one more is coming) well in hand, I hope he can join a Kiwanis club."

That one letter, it is a pleasure to report, caused the directors of the young husband's firm to take notice of him. Within the year he was chosen as superintendent of production, and next year made a branch manager. That year, too, he not only joined a new Kiwanis club, but was elected president of it. He discovered that "We Build" is not a sentimentalized motto which a bunch of fuddy-duddies may have adopted, but is a guide for action, followed by many of the most influential and successful men of his town and nation.

CHAPTER TEN

SOMEBODY CARES

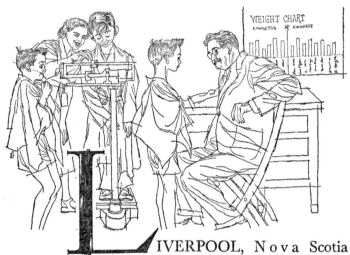

LIVERPOOL, N o v a Scotia
offers an instance of club service to youth which is
so typically Canadian—and American—that it may
well be used to point up the whole Kiwanis program.

Liverpool is not one of the bigger cities, its club
not one of those impressive for sheer number of
members. Moreover, club reports to headquarters
had been somewhat unsatisfactory; the secretary himself, a bit conscience stricken, had written a note of
apology. It was evident, from the tone of the report,
that the members felt a bit ashamed for not having
done more. Nevertheless, the General Office learned
of one item.

A little girl in Liverpool had been critically burned
when she fell onto a stove. The injury was such that
her facial disfigurement was shocking. She lived, but
as she grew older she began to realize the horror of

her burned countenance. It so affected her that it was ruining her life. She was even driven to the point of planning suicide. But a Kiwanian learned about her and reported to his club.

"It will take about $500 to get her to Montreal for an examination and initial operation," said he. "Do we have that much money for this purpose?"

"I move we send her at once, regardless of what our treasury holds," someone spoke up.

"Second the motion!" came as a chorus, an acclamation.

They understood the situation. If there was insufficient money, as of now, it would nevertheless appear in due time. It always has, they knew, when such a challenge was accepted; it always will. The little girl was sent to the specialist. And back came the report.

"It will be necessary," the club was told, "to perform not one but several operations on her. And the cost will go much higher than $500."

"Move it be done at once."

"Second the motion."

Again it was by acclamation. By faith.

And so, as the months passed, a distinguished plastic surgeon completely re-made that child. Gradually, skillfully, he restored her physical well-being. It took *twenty-three operations!* And the cost, even at a cut rate, ran out of the hundreds and into the thousands of dollars.

But when the job was finished, there she stood, happy and bright with hope. The unsightliness had been turned into physical beauty. The Kiwanians went a step further and got her a job. Morale climbed back to where it should be in youth. Gratitude could never be fully expressed, never be shown; no human agency on earth can ever repay the good turn done there, and no repayment was expected.

Indeed, the Kiwanians were still shamed a little because, they felt, their service record hadn't been as full as it might be. They did not dwell on the success of the girl's case. They simply reported it very briefly as a part of routine, and at the end added—"This case is now closed."

*　　*　　*

One year the International Board of Trustees dictated a single objective in the Kiwanis action program that became one of the most important of all. The current phrasing of it is: *"Inspire hope— let each handicapped or delinquent youth know 'Someone cares'."*

Inspire hope!

It is a divine command if ever there was one. And more Kiwanis leaders have hearkened to it than to any other. Yet the very nature of the action required here is such that no statistical report, no summary, no adequate record of any kind can be possible.

"My own dad never pays much attention to me," said one boy, "but you *wanted* me."

He was addressing the Kiwanian who, sonless himself, had simply borrowed a neighbor lad to take to a routine father-and-son meeting.

And what came of it? Nothing, for the official records. Nothing, indeed, that the man's fellow clubmen ever heard about. The man simply kept on "wanting" the lad. Began to study him and his problem, and by degrees—it sometimes takes infinite tact and patience to render a heart service—he began to work on the boy's father. The father, he learned, had long been harassed and miserable in his work. He had an adequate income, but was a misfit at earning it, so much so that nerves were frayed, tempers short, and the entire home unhappy. The Kiwanian found it relatively easy to steer the man into a better occupation. And in time, to guide father and son into the companionship that both craved.

*   *   *

Inspire hope?

What is hope? The little girl so insufferably burned in Liverpool, Nova Scotia had no hope! Until somebody who cared stepped in.

A desperately poor woman in La Feria, Texas had no hope. Until Kiwanians hired an airplane to drop non-denominational cards inviting and urging everybody to attend church. One fell into her tub as she was washing, and—so eager are we to grasp at life —she considered it a miracle, a sign from on high. So she did go to church, and made her needs known, so that the "somebody who cared" could give the aid they wanted to give.

But the Kiwanians in the deep South who decided to look into "the race problem" had no such dramatic experience. One of the club committeemen simply stood up one day in meeting and said, "Gentlemen, I've been checking on the families we helped last Christmas with groceries and such. One of them is still pretty bad off. The father is still sick, and his little kids are getting hungry."

"What did you do about it?" another member asked.

"I fed them. They won't need anything more right now. But next month—"

"I'll take them next month," the second member spoke up again. "Is anybody in the family able to work?"

"The mother is. But her hands are full nursing the father and minding eleven kids."

"I'll take the next month."

"Give me the next." . . . "I'll take a month." . . . "One here."

All that while, nobody thought to ask if the family was white or colored. Nobody was interested in that. That sort of volunteer speak-up began to assail the committeeman. He assigned a six-month care period, and said he would re-assign then if necessary. Other hands were still up. The men agreed to do more than just furnish food. They were to check on clothing, housing, medical attention, even recreation and school.

This case was closed in late fall when the grateful father of that family, in good health again, brought in two bushels of yams.

"Jes' hol' on to these heah," he suggested, smiling broadly, "ontil me and my bigges' boys can take de dogs out tonight. We aims to git you some meat."

If you have never lived down South you can't begin to appreciate the value of the meat they got. Some honestly believe that no man has really lived until he has had his fill of sweet 'taters and possum cooked in deep Dixie. The mother cooked the meal, the father served it. It all happened in the Fellowship Room of a little local church. Over the door a sign even says "Fellowship." It is aptly named.

*　　*　　*

The underprivileged child situation is never quite the same from town to town, state to state, province to province. In Canada the acute need one winter may be for clothing. In the Mexican border region, kids don't need to bother much about clothes but need other things. One Kiwanian, a widower in San Diego, "adopted" six Mexican youngsters who were suddenly orphaned. In time it developed that they had a wealthy aunt in Mexico City, but they had no knowledge of her address. He put a tracer after her, located her and told the orphans' story.

"For the very goodness me, senor!" she cried. "I had no idea this have occur. I have not leev in your countree for seex year, and have not hear from my brother, who died. Why wass I not tol'?"

She had more to say. She said it so charmingly that she completely diverted the Kiwanian's attention from his philanthropy. And while it is seldom within the scope of Kiwanis service to guarantee wives to members, it is nevertheless a pleasure to report that the senora, herself a widow, became the foster mother of the kids the Kiwanian had adopted.

*　　*　　*

One of the big Kiwanis clubs in big-hearted Texas received a hurry call on a wintry day. It came from the local welfare workers.

"An emergency has come up," the call said. "We have need for about 200 blankets to keep some of our citizens from suffering. Will you help?"

The club men went into action. Buying 200 new blankets was no strain because the club treasury was sound. Distributing them brought some revealing experiences. Most of these Kiwanians had thought that the club's charity efforts were limited to children. But among the first "customers" encountered was an elderly Negro woman.

"Praise de Good Lawd!" she literally shouted. "For He has sent you heah!"

She may have been right. At any rate the club man on this case discovered that Aunt Mandy had been facing deep cold with only one blanket, shredded and patched with cotton rags. She was given full care.

Two other Kiwanis blankets went to a seventy-five-year-old man crippled with arthritis. He, too, tried to say thank you, but could only mumble, so touched was he. His only bed covering theretofore had been pieces of vegetable sacking crudely sewed together.

But there were many children to be helped, too. Still another of those club men drove up to a home—if it could be called that—where a mother had four small sons, all sleeping on pieces of worn rags. Given their blankets, they were popeyed with wonder and happiness that such luxury could be!

Finally, there was a crippled boy who had to propel himself around in a rickety little wagon that he had acquired. Investigation showed that he was sleeping in his clothing and using newspapers for cover. Two blankets to him became like two million dollars would to most of us.

These are routine experiences, not just in Texas but wherever Kiwanis is found. Development of club charities has been constant, even though Kiwanis definitely is not an "organization for charity." Men who can qualify for membership in such an organization soon discover or reaffirm a secret — that "charity" is an inapt word, that "sharing" is better, and that the sharing brings the most thrilling satisfaction any human being can possibly know. It is that willingness to share, individually and collectively, which is the inner strength of all service organizations. Close study of Kiwanis history reveals that the club pioneers, away back yonder before 1920, began to discover these basic spiritual facts. It reveals also that Kiwanis has prospered most, grown most in numbers and prestige, in those years when the sharing was heaviest. Human nature being what it is, not much can be said about this development in "open meeting"; men just don't like to brag of their good deeds, usually won't even discuss them. Hence the average Kiwanian has no conception of the sharing that Kiwanians really do.

The sharing—of life's bounties—is likely to take any form. Look for instance at the fifteen-year-old Italian refugee that a club in Kansas encountered. This lad was arrested on a charge of entering the United States illegally. His mother had been killed in Italy during the war; his father's whereabouts was unkown. The boy positively *knew* that he would now be shot to death, for that is what happened to people arrested in Mussolini's Italy.

"No, sonny," his appointed Kiwanian counselor tried to explain. "Arrest here doesn't mean execution. You will not be hurt. You will be fed and clothed and given a bed. And, sonny — you have friends. Understand? Friends. I am one of them."

It was hard to understand, even when it was translated. Why would a strange man, and other strange men whom he had never seen be called his friends?

A way was found to keep the lad in this country legally, and then the Kiwanians went to work on him. The town had an Italian colony, so he was given a place in a suitable Italian home. An Italian priest was induced to teach him English and help acquaint him with the American way of life. Kiwanians tactfully discarded his dirty, worn clothing and replaced it with warm garments—with spending money in the pockets. Other Kiwanians—those "friends" whom he couldn't envision at first — escorted him to church, to school, to playgrounds, and began a gradual vocational counseling. Within a year he was well on the way to becoming a substantial and happy American citizen.

"And if there is any more thrilling experience than helping reclaim this boy," a Kiwanian said, in a heart-felt report to his club committee one day, "I can't imagine what it is. I for one haven't been doing enough of this sort of thing. From now on, I shall make it my own pattern of life, for the sheer joy it brings."

*   *   *

Among the most stirring of all Kiwanis projects since the organization began is that developed by the club at Spokane, Washington.

In 1925 Kiwanians there discovered that many widows with children were having extremely hard times. The men set out to provide homes for them. But no communal or institutionalized dwelling was set up. Instead, separate cottages were purchased or built, and one family put into each at very low rental. Thus the children and their mother could live approximately a normal life.

Since that beginning, twenty-seven such homes have been acquired and put into service. If a widow marries, she moves out. For those who stay, there is hope even of having their places rent free; when the rent money paid in equals the cost of the home, she stops paying. Kiwanians maintain the properties, doing much of the repair and upkeep with their own hands.

More than 42 boys and girls were in those Kiwanis homes at this writing. The Spokane club men also have an educational fund to help such of their "adopted" children as need it. Many of the Kiwanians act as Big Brothers to the youngsters, who often are guests at outings at the Kiwanis Health Center—eighty acres on the Little Spokane River.

This remarkable service project has achieved international renown, and justifiably so. One incident attests to the approval that the citizens of Spokane have put on it. The door man at the hotel where Kiwanis meets died suddenly. In his will he gave his own home to the club, as one more to help in the care of the widows and fatherless children.

Often a Kiwanis service project for youth snowballs itself into greatness before the Kiwanians realize it. That was true of the "Sand Lot" Baseball League which the club men in New York State launched in 1944.

"If we work at this thing," one optimist said, "we can develop a league of boys totaling at least 2000."

Some of his club fellows grinned, but backed him anyway. Next year he did the grinning. His league —*their* league—had 383 teams and 7155 players in just twelve months!

Even that was only a beginning. Today the figure is at 1584 teams, with 26,858 boys actively playing!

Incredible popularity of the league focused attention of all Kiwanis on it. If that's a way to help our youths grow into wholesome citizens, then we're for it, the club men began saying.

In four years the league in New York became a million-dollar project. Some players had graduated to the big leagues. One was signed by the Dodgers at a bonus of $30,000. Another was in the Yankee lineup.

Sports lovers, and people who are fond of children, have been watching this project from all over the continent. For it seems to be proving that "A boy in a ball game is a boy out of trouble."

*   *   *

The sheer variety of services that Kiwanis has rendered to young people and children is astonishing. Studying them is the most fascinating phase of Kiwanis history. Here, in capsule form, are a few more typical exhibits.

A four-year-old boy in St. Louis was stricken with an ailment which doctors said would take his life in a few months. And his parents had spent every dime, even to selling their personal effects, to take care of him. Kiwanis heard of it and stepped in.

"I don't care about nothin' else only I wish I could have a 'lectric train for Christmas," the little fellow said.

He had it, and everything else that could be done for him, via a big plump Kiwanis Santa Claus.

Kiwanians in an Oklahoma town heard about a school girl who had unusual talent and needed help with her music lessons. They furnished the help, even to sending her to New York for study. Then she met a chap who married her and made good for her in the business world, and even did much better than the average man in politics. Name of their protegee today is Mrs. Thomas L. Dewey.

Literally hundreds of Kiwanis clubs have helped schools buy band uniforms and instruments. Typical is the club that sponsored the Cutler-Orosi High School band in California. School authorities failed to authorize purchase of band uniforms, but the year-old Kiwanis club stepped in and raised $1000 for them. Then it embarked on a project to discover and encourage musical talent among the students by means of contests, with prizes of scholarships at outstanding conservatories.

And a Kiwanian in New Mexico sent a piano 116 miles to a Navajo Indian's hogan, when he learned that the Indian's daughter showed great promise in music.

In Salt Lake City Kiwanians sponsored a $50,000 headquarters for boys and girls clubs. The project included land and construction of a four-story building, and providing of leisure-time activities under qualified adult leadership. Each club there is governed by the youngsters, who elect their separate presidents, council, committees, police, judge, jury, and whatever other agencies are needed. The building contains a 350-seat auditorium, a gymnasium, meeting rooms, hobby rooms, craft shops, and short wave radio station.

Three sight-saving classes are operated by Kiwanians in Miami, Florida for children with such low vision that they cannot obtain an education with ordinary school facilities. Specially trained teachers, brilliant illumination and books printed in large type are provided. Kiwanis provided one teacher with a $350 scholarship to Columbia University to equip her to teach this class. The Miami club has spent nearly $3000 on classroom equipment.

In Washington, D. C. Kiwanians sponsor two to four clinics for crippled children each month and the clinics often are carried to surrounding communities. The patients receive visits from a nurse as well as hospital visits. Conferences with parents and patients, health and social workers, are arranged to adjust individual cases. All fees for examinations, treatments, hospitalization, nursing, supervision, medicines and orthopedic supplies are paid by the club.

For more than a quarter-century Kiwanians in Los Angeles have actively supported the McKinley Home for Boys. Its facilities include a playground and tennis courts, under lights, and the club a few years ago added an $85,000 gymnasium. The club also gives each boy a ten-day outing at a camp built especially for McKinley Home youngsters.

Camp Allen for blind and visually handicapped

girls is maintained by Kiwanians of Boston. Many new improvements are added to the camp each year; these have included a water storage tank, a refrigerator and stove, a new lodge, radio, sewing machine, electric clock and iron. Sixty or more girls attend the camp each year.

Crippled and underprivileged children in McPherson, Kansas benefit each year from Kiwanians' "Pancake Festival."

This unique event has come to be enjoyed by the townsfolk as much as by the club men. Kiwanians themselves prepare and serve the cakes. One typical year the citizens consumed 452 pounds of pancake flour, 113 pounds of butter, forty-five pounds of syrup, forty-five dozen eggs, twenty-one pounds of shortening, eighty-four gallons of skim milk, 750 half-pints of drinking milk and thirty-one quarts of coffee cream. The children's fund netted $900. McPherson is a town of less than 10,000 population.

In Harrisburg, Pennsylvania particular stress has been laid on developing "Kiwanis Knights." This is an organization to aid boys who need a bit of romance in life, as well as physical aids. One instance there points up the whole program. A boy named John ———— lived with poor parents and seven brothers and sisters in the town's low-rent area. Unfortunate circumstances led him into thievery, so that by the time he was eight years old he was a gang leader. His gang was arrested and sent to reform school. When John was released he began once more to drift. Then a Kiwanian invited him to become a Kiwanis Knight.

Knighthood, as practiced there, means simply a wholesome environment and guidance, with Kiwanis supplying the direction. Respectability gradually took root in the lad. At the outset of World War II, he enlisted and served honorably in the Navy. After discharge he re-entered school and prepared himself for the ministry, married and began rearing a family of his own. He has repeatedly given public tribute to the Kiwanians who reclaimed his life.

The Kiwanis clubs in Greater Toronto, Ontario have combined their energies to stage an annual "Musical Miracle" which is unique in public service efforts. The festival offers two solid weeks of music — morning, afternoon and evening. Thousands of individual singers and instrumentalists take part. They range in age from five to seventy. In addition to competing for awards, each musician's performance is carefully analyzed by experts, and criticisms made for improvement.

In Albuquerque, New Mexico Kiwanians found that potentially "delinquent" boys needed only to have a physical and spiritual lift to be set on the road toward good citizenship. So the men established a genuine boys ranch, with horses, cattle, all the fascinating things that a ranch offers, plus a set of adult leaders who put love above discipline.

Kiwanis Big Brothers have developed in many clubs throughout the nation, to afford guidance to youngsters paroled from detention homes or other institutions of correction, and especially to help those who are in danger of so-called delinquency. They work with police and other authorities, confer with mothers clubs and schools, and assist wherever there is an opportunity. This has proved to be one of the most delightful forms of Kiwanis service.

*   *   *

Hearing aids, seeing-eye dogs, Braille textbooks, eye glasses, beds, X rays, therapeutic lamps, wheel chairs, braces, literally anything needed to work toward physical normalcy are provided as required by needy children in almost every town where there is a Kiwanis club.

It would be possible — and inspiring — to relate literally thousands of heart stories about Kiwanis service to needy people. They are the stories that do *not* get into the official records. The average Kiwanian learns of them in casual conversation with his fellows, or through newspaper or radio reports. Most Kiwanians want little or no publicity on their community service accomplishments. But let those people who view the American character with alarm, those who foresee doom because our citizens are "selfish," quail before the quiet strength of men to whom service and love are not just words but are guides for living.

And let us now inspect one more heart story, the one that has become classic in Kiwanis history and that is likely to be re-told for its sheer beauty all down the years. It is perhaps best related by one man who was Kiwanis' own scribe, Roe Fulkerson. He has it in his book, *My Personal Pages*. Here is his version:

I had a fat friend who agreed with other members of his Kiwanis club to transport some underprivileged children to hospitals and fresh air camps. One day he had troubles. Things broke wrong and he was taking it on the chins. He had half a dozen, and he was taking it on all of them at once. While he was holding a one-man lodge of sorrow for his own benefit, the secretary of the club telephoned to ask him to take a crippled child to the hospital.

The operation was scheduled for nine o'clock and the hospital was fifty miles away. He was in no humor to get up at seven in the morning and get a confounded kid and take it to a hospital! He was as busy as a young lady centipede putting on her stockings, and mad besides!

But, anyway, he went. A woman came out of the little house with a child in her arms, put it on the front seat beside him and mumbled her thanks through her tears. He said everything would be all right and drove almost a block before he spoke to the child. There looking up at him was a pair of big brown eyes such as one sees only in the faces of hunting dogs and sick children.

"You are God, aren't you, mister?" said the child.

"I'm afraid not, little feller," said the fat man.

"But Mother was praying beside my bed, and she said that God would help me get to the hospital so I can get well and play baseball and go swimming like other boys. So you *must* be God!"

CHAPTER ELEVEN

A TOWN REBORN

WHILE THE FIRST heart appeal to Kiwanians doubtless will always be in working with young people, this is by no means the sum of Kiwanis service, or even the beginning of it.

"Our first aim always," said one of the 1917 convention orators, "must be that of reciprocal trade, one club member with another."

Such clannish selfishness was promptly ruled out in favor of a much broader service concept. Over three decades, therefore, Kiwanis has been emphasizing the spiritual or "human" values. This has now reached incredible proportions. It resulted not from any lofty decree handed down by the International Board of Trustees, but from a ground swell of sentiment among members everywhere.

It is no longer necessary to stress high-level business dealings between Kiwanians; the club men today are almost automatically ethical. They do not become Kiwanians, or stay Kiwanians, if they are guilty of questionable conduct in their respective businesses and professions. It can be assumed in almost every instance that if a man is a Kiwanian, he also is a gentleman.

The mid-century emphasis, therefore, is in service to community, state and nation in almost every possible way. For themselves Kiwanians ask only an hour and a half to two hours of fellowship once a week. In activity they think first of children—and the preceding chapters can barely hint of the work they do with young Americans and Canadians—then they turn to public affairs. During the past twenty-odd years, but especially since the victory in 1945, this has been manifest by an increasing determination to get Americans to the election polls; they have been fighting the strange and dangerous apathy which besets those of us who have the right to vote.

"I have made a person-by-person check-up of the men in this club," one president announced to his fellows, just after a state election, "and of our 106 members, only twenty-nine voted. Forty-six of us couldn't vote, having failed to register."

He shamed them mercilessly. And he kept it up so that at the next opportunity—a municipal election —every Kiwanian and every adult in every Kiwanian's family went to the polls.

A study as to *why* leading, conscientious citizens have been negligent about voting, is too involved for presentation here. But it is not too involved for Kiwanis to take up as a major objective, and it has been so recognized. Recent history of Kiwanis through the two nations shows decided improvement, not only in "getting out the vote" of Kiwanians themselves, but in leading other citizens to the polls. In addition, Kiwanians have been working on the matter of getting qualified men to run for office, and of getting accurate information about candidates and issues before the general public. Lack of sufficient information caused Kiwanis to go into action at Poplar Bluff, Missouri. A careless public there had voted down a mill tax to raise teachers' pay, even though teachers were getting less than clerks.

"Our study of that vote shows how few people understood the true situation," the Kiwanis committee reported to its club. "We recommend, therefore, that we Kiwanians dedicate ourselves to informing the public, and see to it that another election is called."

It was done, and the raise for teachers received a tremendous vote.

But then, there is the Kiwanian in the southern town of 5000 population, who led an aggressive campaign to re-elect the town's mayor.

"He has served us admirably for five terms," the Kiwanian orated, wherever he had the chance. "He deserves the honor of a sixth term. I hope nobody runs against him. We have a high type man in office, so let us see to it that he is kept there."

The club man was so much in earnest about supporting his friend that he worked night and day on it, never realizing, at the same time, what *his* friends were doing. Led by the incumbent mayor, the Kiwanian's friends conducted a quiet house - to - house counter-campaign — and put the Kiwanian in as mayor by a write-in vote of more than forty to one! Such is the beautiful measure of friendships in small towns.

*   *   *

"Public affairs" is a term subject to broad interpretation and application. Wherefore, there is no strict limit on what a club can do in this category. In Pittsburgh, for instance, it took the form of a horse show. Records for just one year indicate the success of it—$20,000 was netted and turned over to the Rheumatic Fever Foundation of that city. But almost every city and town where Kiwanis meets can point to one or more concrete improvements that the club men bring about each year. Libraries have been established, and books purchased for others. Quick-freeze and cold storage facilities have been developed, city planning groups established, symphony orchestras organized. In one town Kiwanis provided pulmotors for the fire department. In another, the effort was a house-to-house canvass to secure X-ray tests for tuberculosis, and in still another it was an extensive mosquito and fly eradication campaign. Iron lungs are bought, health units established, tree planting campaigns started.

Many state governors and ex-governors are Kiwanians, as are hundreds of mayors and other elected officials. Former President Truman was a charter member of the Kiwanis Club of Independence, Missouri. A survey of the Eighty-fifth Congress revealed that one out of every six members of the House and Senate is affiliated with a Kiwanis club.

Dramatic stories by the dozens could be selected in the field of public affairs. The big cities afford no end of them. But for good down-to-earth application of Kiwanis idealism, few communities have exceeded the town of McLouth, Kansas.

A sign on the outskirts of McLouth says: Population 500. That could be slightly in error either way. A while back some of its citizens realized that it lacked much of perfection. They would huddle in the post office about it, or in the grocery or church. They knew of Kiwanis, and one of McLouth's leading businessmen was delegated to write for information covering the formation of a new club.

"It will take a minimum of twenty-five top men, all community leaders, with only two from any one profession or type of work," they were told. McLouth's men got busy and shot back an answer.

"We have carefully selected our men," they reported. "Each one has been screened as to ability and integrity. Can you help us organize now?"

Headquarters could. And thirty-seven men were chartered in that new Kiwanis club. Moreover, they accepted the charter and immediately started a program of activity.

*   *   *

McLouth had no doctor. The Kiwanians looked through Kansas City and Topeka, located a good one, and induced him to move to McLouth. They then discovered they had no home for him, so they worked fast again and raised $15,000 to buy living quarters and an office. Thus the first public affairs effort was completed in record time to still a crying need.

McLouth had no druggist. It is unthinkable in America for a good homey town not to have a "corner drug," a pharmacist who can be nicknamed Doc, and who can take his high place in the life there. Kiwanians again scoured the county and brought home a good one.

Need for a town dentist became apparent, so the club men took on the responsibility of getting him, too.

More electric power was needed, so they worked through R. E. A and got that.

These things were not accomplished easily. Nor were they accomplished by the Kiwanians alone. The club men sparked the efforts but the whole citizenry backed them. Especially did the women of McLouth help. The wife of the new Kiwanis club president was herself president of the local Garden Club and she led her group into the campaign. If truth be known—and it too seldom is in such instances—the women of Kiwanis often are responsible for what their men achieve.

*   *   *

It is a vital part of North American tradition to boast of being "a country boy come to town." Even if, literally speaking, a man has scarcely ever been out of the shadow of the Empire State Building, he has a yearning inside him for the soil.

This fundamental urge has made Kiwanis service to agriculture of major importance over the years. Before Kiwanis was one-year-old many of its members were giving direct personal aid in emergency harvesting of crops. By 1920 it was a standard service for Kiwanians to sponsor and encourage farm youths. How? No limit has been set, nor will be.

Listen to the gangly backwoodsy boy of sixteen down in Kentucky: "I never knowed no man in town would want to come and help me. Now I aim to raise hawgs twicet as good." A Kiwanian had simply spotted him at a rural school program, paid him a friendly visit and loaned him ten dollars to buy a better boar.

Officially, however, it was back in 1922 when International President Harry E. Karr of Baltimore, a lawyer, began stressing the building of closer relations between "country men and town men." He held, correctly, that the only important difference between them was that one group wore comfortable clothing and lived in the open air, while the others wished they did. In business they were not—or need not be — antagonistic; they had every reason and ability to cooperate. Bringing the two groups together for the common good thus became a major objective of Kiwanis at President Karr's urging.

"Kiwanians have long believed," another club executive wrote, "that the economy of our nations is dependent upon our national resources, and that the farmer is the custodian or administrator of much of those resources. With this in mind, Kiwanis as an International organization has developed a broad Action Program to improve rural-urban relations."

Literally hundreds of thousands of farm workers have been brought into communities by Kiwanians, as the need arose. Thousands of special meetings, speakers, soil and crop experts, farm and farm home activity leaders, have been provided. One club swapped a hive of bees to a farmer for a bucket of honey later. Rural electrification programs developed by

Kiwanis are common. Kiwanis-sponsored groups of Future Farmers of America, Junior Farmers, 4-H Clubs, farm and livestock fairs, harvest festivals, poultry shows, and such, began when Kiwanis was in its infancy. Now they number into the thousands annually, and are a routine part of almost every club's service program.

*   *   *

Business Standards is an activity field which appeals to all Kiwanians. Joe Prance, the first Kiwanian, was directly interested in improving the standards in his home town, Detroit. Joe expressed the opinion that, "Somebody ought to put pressure on businessmen who do cheap things."

Somebody did. As of mid-century there are several organized groups who watch over business firms to keep them in line. And the best part of it is, any one of them can draft all the others for mass pressure as required. The part of Kiwanis in this is relatively small, for it determined forty years ago not to "meddle," not to moralize. But the prestige wallop that Kiwanis packs is enough to make any unethical businessman fearful. The Kiwanis approach to the matter has been one of education rather than correction and punishment. To that end, open forums on business practices were started years ago. Virtually every club in the great organization now conducts at least one business standards program each year for its own members. Forums for the public extend beyond that. Labor-management relations have become a main educational study. Many instances are on record showing how Kiwanis clubs served as arbiters in industrial difficulties, how they restored waning good will, how they influenced that ultimate and greatest weapon of all—public opinion—toward getting one faction or another into its proper groove. When clubs and communities are small, the service effort is likely to be an humble one because most of the leading business and professional men will be a part of Kiwanis itself.

*　　*　　*

Kiwanians render public affairs service *in addition to* their work as club men which sets them apart as a legion of leaders under the American and Canadian flags. The average member must have shown this kind of selflessness before being invited to join Kiwanis in the first place. (Membership is by invitation only.) Conceivably he might slump, or might at least transfer his efforts and energies to club service alone, once he became a member. But away back in the history of the organization, any such tendency began to be taboo. At the Birmingham convention in 1919 a speaker warned the members — "We do not simply change our field of service to humanity when we join a Kiwanis club nor in any way lighten our load. We take on more!" That was true then, and has become increasingly true over the forty years since.

A survey of club members showed that 69.4 per cent were serving on one or more community boards and commissions, in addition to work in Kiwanis. Inevitably that percentage will vary from week to week, always, but most of the variance over the years has been a steady climb. Here were some of the specific ways in which Kiwanians were doing community service outside their clubs:

School boards	10.8%
Recreation commissions	10.6%
Safety commissions	5.6%
Hospital boards	8.9%
Church boards	38.1%
(*Church attendance by Kiwanians is nearer* 80%)	
Airport commissions	1.8%
Public utilities	2.5%
Streets and highways	2.6%
Parks and playgrounds	4.8%
Health boards	7.5%
Community chests	13.0%
Miscellaneous	20.8%

*   *   *

Mankind was never so happily inspired as when it made a cathedral.   —STEVENSON

From its very beginning Kiwanis has built on a foundation of reverence for God. This fact surprises the cynics and the sophisticates outside the organization. Even many church people misunderstand, saying that the "luncheon" clubs would do better if they quit eating so much and served God more. They speak in pure ignorance. In the final analysis, the success of Kiwanis and all kindred groups is due to the fact that the entire program is one of unselfish, godly service. There is no denominationalism, no sectarianism, no theology as such. But almost one hundred per cent of Kiwanians are church-minded men, and almost eighty per cent are active in regular church work. Literally thousands of church officers in America and Canada wear the lapel button of Kiwanis, and many hundreds of ministers, priests and rabbis.

It is significant, therefore, that Kiwanis International has found wide interest in that division of service called Support of Churches in Their Spiritual Aims. This was made an official part of the International program in 1935-36 when Harper Gatton, a Kentuckian, was Kiwanis president. It was a timely move. America had been shocked out of materialistic thinking by the worst depression since Civil War times, and was beginning to look toward deeper concepts. Kiwanis was no exception. And yet, very early in Kiwanis history it became apparent to most leaders that emphasis should be placed on the spiritual.

"We *could* support merely the building of new temples, aid in the purchase of pipe organs and pews and such," an earlier president, Victor M. Johnson, said. "But we had better adopt a policy that transcends the dollar and gets us closer to God." He was, of course, right, yet the acceptance of such wisdom always comes slowly. Much more has been said about this in club meetings since the world holocaust of the early 1940's, and so at mid-century the Number One Object of Kiwanis is "To give primacy to the human and spiritual, rather than to the material values of life."

The detailed way in which this has taken form is beyond the scope of a one-volume history, indeed would be elusive to any historian with unlimited space, because most spiritual service cannot be reported in words, since it is of the emotions, the heart. Nevertheless here are a few statistics as taken from actual reports of clubs and they are very revealing:

Nearly 95,000 religious advertisements were sponsored.

More than 25,000 "Go to Church" campaigns were conducted.

4,884 lay preachers were provided for churches.

Over 25,000 Kiwanians taught Sunday School classes or assisted in Weekday Religious Education.

Nearly $400,000 was raised and/or contributed for special church funds.

Over 500,000 "Prayer Before Meals" table tents were distributed in public eating places.

There are no statistics of personal church calls made by Kiwanians. And no way to show in cold figures what effect a typical Inter-Faith Council had on people in Chicago.

This Council, organized by the Lake View Kiwanis club, consisted of the heads of Protestant and Catholic churches and of Jewish synagogues, and two lay members from each congregation. In public forums, prejudices were aired and ended, mutual problems of all kinds solved. More than 1500 people crowded in to hear or take part at each meeting.

Such councils—sometimes under other names—have been developed in many regions by Kiwanians. Often the forum discussions are brought before club meetings. Back in 1938 a "Radio Forum of Better Understanding" was begun by Kiwanians in Fresno, California, with Catholic, Jewish and Protestant faiths all represented by distinguished men. It became one of the area's best loved programs. Comparable work has been done over many another radio station by Kiwanians. Kiwanis itself holds hundreds of top radio executives, who have been of immeasurable help in this extension of spiritual service.

"Practically speaking, radio and Kiwanis are about the same age," one executive said. "I became a Kiwanian shortly after I established my first radio station, and immediately saw the possibilities of linking the two in public service. With the Church as a guide, I have continued this work over the years."

Kiwanis continued its support of spiritual concepts when Ben Dean of Grand Rapids was International President in 1944-45. President Dean was no minister. He was an advertising executive, and as such was attuned to America's heart throbs as few men ever are. Through his knowledge of public relations all service groups rose greatly in public esteem, and a major part in that campaign was simply to let people know that Kiwanis does put spiritual concepts first.

President Dean spoke "officially" for Kiwanis in that regard once without realizing it. He did it in a conventional but delightful American way. Sitting around a campfire with a group of friends in Michigan he told a story. When he was urged to tell it again before the Kiwanis Club of New York City, he did it so effectively that a celebrated columnist was moved to devote his entire syndicated column to it. Here is the story:

One Sabbath a professor of speech at a Scottish university visited a friend in a small village. During the morning service in the kirk the host rose from his seat in the congregation and said, "Pastor, we have in the congregation this morning a distinguished professor of speech from our neighboring university. Would you like to have him recite the Twenty-third Psalm?"

"By all means," said the pastor, and the professor went to the platform and recited the matchless Psalm of the Shepherd. He did it with such feeling and richness of voice that the people were visibly moved.

After he had returned to his seat, someone in the congregation rose and said, "And now, pastor won't you, too, please read the Psalm?"

And so the venerable pastor, who had spent years in their midst, and knew their joys and sorrows from a lifetime of love and labor among them, in his tired old voice repeated those golden words of faith and promise.

As the professor and his host walked homeward after church, the host said, "Did you notice what a strange thing happened? When you repeated the Psalm so feelingly the congregation was visibly moved. But when the pastor spoke the same words, there was hardly a dry eye. Why was that?"

The professor, who must have been a modest and discerning man, replied, "Why, that is easy. You see, I know the Psalm, but the pastor knows the Shepherd."

CHAPTER TWELVE

"WHAT RIGHT TO LIVE?"

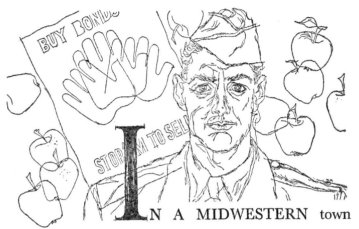

IN A MIDWESTERN town on the morning of June 10, 1939, the president of a bank picked up his telephone.

"Jim? This is Ed," said he, when the connection was made. "Look," Ed continued, "I've been thinking. Remember how we drilled for a month with wooden rifles, getting ready for the Kaiser? Well, how about us getting our sons out now, say two evenings a week?"

"Do you have the wooden rifles?" Jim asked.

"No. But the bank has a mortgage on that new woodworking shop down near the railroad. I bet if I asked them they'd let us use their saws. We could have, say, coffee and pie some night—the women would fix it—and whip out a hundred rifles in no time. Just power saw work, and a little sandpapering."

"Sure, sure! I'd like to do it myself, Ed."

"You were a top sergeant during the last war. Why don't you get a new manual, Jim, and brush up on the drills, eh? I think the boys will enjoy it. Now take my own son—he's nineteen, and a little military training would help smooth off some of the rough edges—"

It developed just that way. It was fun, yet it was serious. June sweated on into July and August. America was double-World's Fair-conscious, Hitler was just a big foreign noise; but the instinct for preparedness — heritage perhaps from pioneering days—was stirring in the breasts of many a business and professional man. And come that fateful autumn, Hitler marched!

Today, Hitler and his world horror are gone, but the banker's handsome son is ex-Captain Gerard Davis Spaulding, living with three little sons of his own in a free land, and a wife who treasures assorted medals that her man won for valor in the infantry. Four-fifths of the 116 young men trained in that small city, first with wooden rifles, became officers soon after Uncle Sam beckoned. Nine of them, along with Ed and Jim, who are older in years but not in spirit, belong to the same Kiwanis club.

Kiwanis enlisted early for service in World War II. As the banker, other astute club officers throughout the United States and Canada were able to read the dark and bloody pages of history before they were written. As far back as 1937, these men were co-operating with earnest Rotarians, Lions and others, trying desperately to change the course of events. When it looked as if war was inevitable, the direction of their efforts took a new turn. Voluntarily they prepared the leadership, helped organize industry, sparked the government itself.

The Allies were not "ready" when Pearl Harbor fell—no nation is ever ready for war—but the essential preliminaries were done. We thus were able in record time to generate the phenomenal production of military materiel, food and other necessities that spelled success. In this great mass effort, service club members occupied key places. The banker's wooden-rifle drill was trivial. Yet great events hinge on little ones. His was multiplied in one form or another a million times over by men of good will everywhere.

"Who will volunteer to serve hamburgers at the servicemen's center each Saturday night?" the Kiwanis president in one town asked. He faced 124 members.

He gave no sales talk, no plea. Yet hands began to rise. In a moment, more than a hundred were up. That club not only served thousands of hamburgers during the next two years, but paid for them as well, in addition to dressing them with pop and coffee, pickles and conversation.

More than 15,000 Kiwanians were in uniform, frequently of high rank because they were already leaders by instinct and training. Many gave their lives. Many more gave their sons, and their daughters. Service at home was beyond estimating. In one eight-month period, Kiwanis clubs sold nearly a billion dollars worth of victory bonds, provided over 80,000 pints of blood to the Red Cross, and collected nearly a million pounds of scrap and over six million pounds of used clothing. Such startling figures could be cited endlessly.

Charles S. Donley, president of Kiwanis International at the start of the war, said, "What right does a service organization have to live if it does not justify its existence? We have never prayed for a war so we could demonstrate our service. But we have been betrayed and attacked. I have offered the trained manpower of Kiwanis to the governments of both the United States and Canada. We are a solid front against the forces of destruction." Enemies and cynics around the globe were to learn the sincerity of that proclamation.

It is now well known that the biggest war plant of all lay just outside the cities, towns and villages of the United States and Canada. That was the factory producing the food necessary to win—the farms of these two nations. Kiwanis farm and garden projects numbered high into the thousands. Bankers and merchants, soil experts and chemists, implement men and transportation leaders, threw their assets behind the man behind the plow. Clubs sponsored large programs and small, marshaling the know-how and the manpower for them. Typical individual effort was that of the quiet Kiwanian in the Southwest who sank his entire personal fortune into four expensive mechanical cotton pickers and planted many thousands of acres to help supply fibre needed for clothing and tires. Victory gardening — small individually, but great in the total production—became a Kiwanis *family* activity in every community for four critical years.

Other club efforts ranged from the building of

morale by aiding war widows and orphans to the building of homes where needy children could live. Some projects were less heart-rending, more spectacular. The Denver Kiwanis club, for example, arranged for the 507th Parachute Infantry to "capture" Denver's municipal airport. This was no mock show, no afternoon of frivolity; it was as realistic as the military men could make it. Huge Army air transports took off from the base at Alliance, Nebraska, arrived over their objective near Denver fifteen seconds ahead of schedule, opened their hatches and dropped 260 troopers. These invaders set up their guns and started firing. A two-pronged pincer movement advanced toward the airport, a half mile from the landing area. The men came in waves, seeking natural shelter as they closed in for the attack. Exactly one hour after the first trooper had "hit the silk," Denver's airport and control towers had been seized. More than 100,000 people saw the staged attack—and under Kiwanis guidance paid for it by donating 10,000 pints of blood to the Red Cross and purchasing many thousands of dollars worth of bonds. Kiwanians and Kiwani-Anns entertained the paratroopers that evening.

St. Thomas, Ontario is a city of less than 18,000 population, but, nevertheless, it contributed more than 2000 gallons of blood from February 1943 to December 1944. The Kiwanis Club of St. Thomas, which directed the program, had planned for 6000 donations a year, but within two months of the holding of the first clinic, the objective had been raised to 7000, then to 9000. Actually, more than 20,000 blood donations were made in twenty-two months.

The club enlisted the aid of 1000 volunteer workers, who, in addition to other duties, served more than 6000 home-cooked meals to Canadian servicemen who made blood donations at the clinic. The club spent more than $14,000 on the project in the period covering less than two years.

In 1939 Hommo J. deKanter, member of the Allentown, Pennsylvania Kiwanis club, went with his family to visit his native Holland. Sudden war trapped them there; not until December 1945 could they return. They faced outrageous privation, until home club members learned of their plight. Then food, clothing and other essentials began to arrive. When a coat for Mrs. deKanter was too heavy to be accepted in the mails, Kiwanis ladies took it apart, mailed it separately, and sent her needles and thread with instructions for putting it together again. The family was cared for during the entire war by packages from friends at home. When he did get back to God's country, Kiwanian deKanter made a special trip to Kiwanis headquarters in Chicago to express his thanks.

One of the outstanding illustrations of Kiwanis participation in America's successful war effort had its beginning in the great apple country of the Pacific Northwest.

The program started with forty apples and came to a successful conclusion several weeks later with nearly $6,500,000 in war bond sales.

It all started when the Spokane club decided to send a box of apples to Hollywood, Florida in the hope that they might be auctioned for at least a twenty-five dollar war bond apiece. What happened came as a surprise because the box brought $5000 in war bond sales, an average of $125 per apple.

Hollywood's experience served as a spring-board for similar sales elsewhere. In fact, eighteen boxes were sent to other clubs. In Dallas, Texas one apple sold for $5000, while the entire box brought $20,550. Sales began to skyrocket as various clubs sought to break Dallas' single-apple merchandising record. Oakland, California reported $6600 for its apple; Chicago, $9075; Pittsburgh, $15,025; Madisonville, Kentucky, $16,625; Omaha, $18,675; and Jersey City went all out with a sale amounting to $25,725.

The parade continued—Los Angeles had a sale of apples that netted $30,650. At Albert Lea, Minnesota, one apple brought $75,000, while the box sold for $126,400. Salt Lake City then topped previous marks with $377,000 for a box.

As the race came into the home stretch, Macon, Georgia sold its box for $1,354,000 and looked as if it would win the contest. So Spokane Kiwanians set out to boost that record. They had some grapefruit painted to resemble Georgia peaches. Before they could auction these peaches, word came from London, Ontario, the home club of International President Fred G. McAlister, that their box of apples had brought $1,556,000 in war bond sales. This challenge, too, was accepted. The final result was a neat little total of $2,787,350 in bonds sold by the Spokane club.

Funds from campaigns such as these financed the guns, tanks, planes and ships with which American and Canadian fighting men conquered the enemy.

On July 4 — American Independence Day — of

1944, a group of Kiwanians made history at Naples. They were Adolph Costella of Santa Cruz, California; Harold E. Wright and H. P. Forsey of Calgary, Alberta; Paul L. Heilman of Picher, Oklahoma; W. E. Stone of Boonville, Missouri; Jack Martin of Shreveport, Louisiana; John McSweeney of Wooster, Ohio, later a member of Congress; Paul Buck of Fairmont, West Virginia; John N. Lummus of Miami, Florida; Samuel O. Hill of Monticello, Florida; John A. Park, Jr., of Raleigh, North Carolina; and William B. Aular of Dunkirk-Fredonia, New York. These twelve sat in a circle, asked God's blessing, sang old familiar songs, heard a colonel and a private in a duet—and talked. Everybody made a short speech, and through it all was a rededication to the Kiwanis ideals of spiritual and physical building. These men knew they would be scattered over Europe within a few hours, perhaps never to meet again, but they shook hands in good will. They were scarcely aware of the symbolic importance of their little session. Theirs had been the first meeting of representatives of any international service organization on foreign liberated soil.

Long before the fighting was over, Kiwanians were building a postwar world. Again their most effective method was an endless series of small efforts. Typical was that of the club in Coeur d' Alene, Idaho. Kiwanians there needed manpower to help erect a big house at their camp for underprivileged children. Italian prisoners of war were stationed nearby, so the club men arranged for thirty of them to help, as volunteers.

"With no sentimentalized fraternizing," said the

club leader, "we allowed those men to share American democracy in action. They worked willingly, and saw our methods in sharp contrast to those of Mussolini. Their reactions were enthusiastically good. The thirty prisoners are better world citizens now for having had one touch of our life."

International officers of Kiwanis had anticipated postwar problems in their own organization and in the two nations served. Special studies by experts were made, and every possible guidance suggestion sent to individual clubs. *Contact,* a regular news folder from Kiwanians on the home front to those in service, had been maintained from the beginning. It had stressed postwar building, as needed. Returned soldiers, whether club members or not, were given every practical aid in readjusting to civilian life—a work destined to continue for years. Reconversion of industry, new efforts in vocational guidance, stronger emphasis on Kiwanis participation and leadership in public affairs of every sort, became the guiding light of the international organization.

For their sacrifices and work in winning the war and building for peace, Kiwanians have asked no bonus, sought no adulation, courted no fame. They are aware that greatest honor cometh within the heart.

CHAPTER THIRTEEN

OUR POST-WAR BUILDING

SHORTLY AFTER victorious warriors returned home to the United States and Canada, they set in with new determination to "win the peace." It was as if The Boys paused for a week to kiss mama and the children, re-establish civilian connections in job and social life and church, then on some bright Monday morning rolled up their sleeves, grinned big and shouted companionably, "Let's get to work!"

They found opportunity beckoning. Scientific advances had been almost incredible — with even grander ones to come. Almost all records had been broken; new population growths, greater production and sales, new superlatives of every kind. The competitive spirit was never so forceful. The cooperative instinct, the teaming of brawn and brain and soul for the common good without sacrifice of individual dignity, had never been so apparent since life began.

Kiwanis not only was a part, it was a leader of this new grandeur. The horror in Europe and Asia had caused all men to search their souls, and the returning soldiers showed a new emotional maturity. Thus certain phenomena were pointed up, which had been treated too lightly theretofore.

It was observed that the greatest advance of the mid-century decade in the United States and Canada was a resurgence of interest in religion, especially in Christianity. When Kiwanis was founded in 1915, only 24 percent of all Americans attended church regularly. By 1956, almost 62 percent of us were attending. ("Regularly" as used here means more than half the Sunday services.) Most of this remarkable increase was achieved in the decade following World War II, and while the rate of it slowed a bit, the increase was still on in 1966. Americans are basically a devout people, a sensible people, who will stomach just so much foolishness, then turn against it. The growth was not just in new churches, increased Sunday School enrollment and outreach, the over-all spiritual tone of the churches rose markedly —this despite the noisy headlines and commentators of the day.

Kiwanis sparked much of that. It was their finest form of Building, following their official motto. The beautiful new booklet, "Kiwanis In Brief," (free from headquarters in Chicago) showed the 1947 Administrative Theme as *Integrity, Leadership, Service*. The very next page of that year's booklet started with this: "Seek ye first . . . This is Our Father's world. We, all of us, are children of God. In mid-twentieth century we are beset by grave problems of community, country and world. They are problems we can serve—but only with God's help." There was more, more deep dedication, ending thus: "As some of His children, in His world, we (Kiwanians) publish our prayer to know His will that it may be done."

Then on Page 2 of that booklet were the Objects of Kiwanis International. The first one reads, "To give primacy to the human and spiritual . . ."

Primacy, mind you; not just lip service, not mere tagalong sop to sentimentality, like a third-rate orator quoting The Bible and waving a flag. This was set by distinguished officers and trustees of an organization then numbering nearly a quarter-million selected men.

There are six of those Objects. They begin thus: "To give . . . To encourage . . . To promote . . . To develop . . . To provide . . . To cooperate." Those are the most potent verbs in any language. They stimulate action of a constructive nature, and reflect the spirit of our motto, "We Build." They are the very essence of spirituality. They are the strong undergirding of the entire Kiwanis International program.

Among the most important and most respected committees in the individual Kiwanis club today is the Committee on Support of Churches in Their Spiritual Aims. In one typical club one year, the chairman of this committee was a Doctor of Philosophy, professor in a college, named Niles Puckett. He happens to be a Baptist. His nine-man committee sat one month at a special table in club meeting so that all might know them well. They included Methodists, Jews, Presbyterians, Catholics, and a Salvation Army major.

Somehow or other they seemed to dominate the entire club programming for the year, not as censors or "Holy Joes" but as pace setters, lending an essential dignity, and quietly pointing to where emphasis should go. Their services included such trivial ones as selecting the men to give the invocation at meetings and choosing Bible verses for the club bulletin. But they also arranged several outstanding club programs including one on — of all things — church humor. Through the membership they collected nearly 100,000 used Christmas Cards for a Christian mission in Korea. They led a Christian vocational guidance effort. They made it almost embarrassing for a Kiwanian not to attend the church of his choice. Their gentle reminders made it easier to recruit men to lead the Community Fund drives, to be Boy Scout and Girl Scout leaders, to sacrifice time and energy in all kinds of humanitarian building. They used spot announcement recordings for broadcast, under such titles as "The New Pilgrimage," "The Way Forward," and "The Power of Prayer." These were supplied by Kiwanis International headquarters.

Dr. Puckett's committee was anything but knife-and-fork, and it was not unique. Since about 1945 the Support of Churches Committees throughout Kiwanis have been implementing those spiritual ideals stated officially by our International trustees.

But where else has the organization made forceful new impact since World War II?

One of course is the Ballot Battalion; Kiwanians getting voters out to the polls. And yet, most of us would surely vote top place to that brand new item in the International program, new at least since the big war. This is the exploration and encouragement of mental health. One of the eight stated official Objectives of Kiwanis International for 1957 read: "Stimulate public understanding of the mental illness problem, and advocate qualified research and professional treatment." Thus again our organization stepped out as a leader.

It was known then, and has since been verified over and over, that more Americans and Canadians are in mental hospitals than are in for treatment of all other ailments combined! Still more would be in hospitals but for lack of room. Others roam the streets, needing treatment but getting none. *One out of twelve* of all citizens at any given moment need treatment for mental ills, hence Kiwanis could find no better place for its Building.

In the 1950's, too, Kiwanians everywhere showed a great new interest in geriatrics—the science of old age. What to do with elderly Mom and Pop has been a problem since Adam began aging. Kiwanians feel that independence of spirit is the keynote of happiness for all elderly folk. Out of this has come a series of "Youngtowns." A Youngtown — actually called that in some instances—is simply a village of and for couples past fifty or so. Each couple has a cottage or apartment, with opportunity for gardening and other hobbies. There is usually a community playground, a recreation hall, even a swimming pool, with everything scaled for minimum expense. But some of the towns are deluxe, for those who can afford to live there. More and more people are living more and more years, hence the problem of how to assimilate "senior citizens" into an increasingly urban society, how to guarantee their contentment with dignity for all, is a growing one. Kiwanis is concerned with this.

At the other end of the age scale, and even more impressive, has been the development of Key Clubs in recent years. First of these was organized at Sacramento, California, High School in 1925. The 1000th Key Club was chartered at Southfield High School, Detroit, on May 1, 1952, and the 20,000th member was installed that year. The 1500th club was chartered at Chatteroy High in Williamson, West Virginia, on December 13, 1956, and the 35,000th member installed that same month. High schools in Newfoundland, Alaska and Hawaii all have Key Clubs. The total number of Key Clubs at press time for this book was 3054, and they had a total of 82,587 members. As always, these youths are not "junior Kiwanians" but are in an autonomous service organization guided by Kiwanis International.

Aside from its heartening statistical growth, the Key Club idea of service has taken hold magnificently. Its program extends beyond the high school and into the community now. Even J. Edgar Hoover rates it as a major help in controlling juvenile delinquency. Key Club influence has commanded attention in several major magazines. The daily press, television, radio, lecturers, schools and churches everywhere have enthusiastically endorsed the youngsters' work. "If Kiwanis had done nothing else in its first fifty years but launch Key Clubs," said one commentator, "it would have justified its existence." In the 1960's a Key Club International Convention seemed as impressive as a Kiwanis International convention. Harken to what one big hotel manager had to say: "By now we are accustomed to adult conventioneers who act like boys. It is refreshing indeed to have boy conventioneers who act like adults."

Circle K International—the comparable organization for college men—in proportion to opportunity has matched Key Club growth. There is a "new climate of opinion" concerning the old, established fraternities in colleges. The purely social organization is not as popular or as common as it used to be; the *service* ideal has been growing, instead. Thus the Circle K groups demonstrate a maturity far above the so-called kooks and beatniks who have made campus noises, but are really of no consequence.

In 1955 Kiwanis initiated Farm/City Week. This became exactly what its name implies—an occasion for renewing and stressing the growing interdependence of rural-urban communities and individuals. The country producer and the town consumer have never been basically different in attitudes and needs. Farm/City programs (usually in November) point up that fact, while re-cementing friendships and building new understanding. This effort has been hailed as one of the top good-will builders of the century.

Close relationship between Kiwanis and the national governments of the United States and Canada has been demonstrated more and more. As early as 1949, Kiwanis International and the Kiwanis Club of Washington, D. C., started a series of deluxe Congressional Dinners. Purpose was to honor publicly the then more than 100 Kiwanians serving in the Senate and House of Representatives. Other such dinners followed, with approval for them shown throughout the nation. Similarly, the Kiwanis Club of Ottawa stages appreciation dinners for Kiwanians in the Canadian National Parliament.

When Kiwanis reached the age of forty years, an observance seemed right and proper to everybody. The year was 1955, and every club in the two nations staged their proper parties. The general public took notice. In the White House itself, President Don E. Engdahl of Kiwanis International and his Board of Trustees called on President Dwight Eisenhower and presented him with a plaque which solemnly stated that "Kiwanis International, through the re-dedication of each of its individual members, pledges itself to an ever broadening service to the communities of the United States."

A similar presentation was made to Prime Minister Louis St. Laurent of Canada, and a Pledge of Re-dedication was presented to many mayors throughout the two countries.

While Kiwanis was busy making awards, it was receiving many more. Freedoms Foundations honored the organization repeatedly — four times, for example, between 1949 and 1955; then in 1956 gave Kiwanis a big special award for its "exceptional service to the American concept of freedom." Many other groups, national and local, have given Kiwanis comparable recognition.

On a bright day in 1949 Kiwanis began formal

observance of Kids' Day. The programming for this varied with individual clubs. Typically, one club of 150 members took 4,200 effervescent boys and girls to an Air Force Base for an air show. This was so successful that it became an annual event. In other cities, kids have been "recognized" in many imaginative and helpful ways, all leading toward higher citizenship.

During that period, too, Canadian Kiwanians developed an enterprise called Crusade For Better Reading, and it spread into the United States. It develops an interest on the part of parents in the types of reading material available to youths.

Further projection of youth training has showed in the Youth Panel Forums. Kiwanian leaders realized that, with all our shouting about the glories of American capitalism, our big children simply had not been told its advantages over communism and socialism. The Forums were designed to correct this, and became highly popular as well as enlightening. A fringe benefit is that thousands of Kiwanians themselves learned valuable pointers.

Recruiting of local school teachers is on the agenda of hundreds of Kiwanis clubs now. The men work with school trustees and other local officials, who themselves often wear the Kiwanis membership pin. Vocational guidance toward teaching is given high school and college youths. The said truth is, at least a fourth of the existing school teachers are known to be misfits, unsuited for teaching; the mere fact of owning a college degree in Education does not prepare a misguided personality for teaching youths. Trying to develop men and women with eagerness, enthusiasm, plus love for the young, is a factor in this programming. The public also is a goal for an educational campaign, making it clear that higher pay for teachers is imperative now.

Countless other Kiwanis projects are under way in the educational category. These include The American Bookshelf, a program designed to build international good will; Honor Citizenship, a project to develop youth leadership; Safety, a critically important effort to encourage individual responsibility; Work and Pray for Permanent Peace, a program based on the feeling that the average citizen must be willing to struggle for a peaceful world just as he would be for success in war, but without sacrificing safety and honor.

In recent years also, a new term came into every Kiwanian's word book—"CQ." The C stands for Citizenship, the Q for Quotient, which of course refers to Quality also. This project began in 1959 and gained momentum fast, with club after club developing novel ways of helping men toward better citizenship while heightening their own. These are just a *few* samples of Kiwanis in action in the past decade. The service achievements of Kiwanis across the world are truly incredible, so vast are they.

The spotlight has been equally bright on numerical growth. With Kiwanis maturing, many clubs now have father and son members, and some have father, son and grandson. This makes a happy teaming of talents. Since about 1954 there has been a definite trend toward the formation of new clubs in metropolitan areas. The population changes in recent years have brought more and more people to cities and larger towns. Kiwanis once had most of its clubs in communities of 10,000 people or less. Now most are in towns of 25,000 or more, because towns are growing so rapidly, and rural areas are changing.

Population growth is Kiwanis' biggest opportunity. At this writing, the United States is crowding up close to 200,000,000 people, with the pace accelerating. Not long ago, research scholars at California Institute of Technology said that unless birth rates are controlled, the world of 1999 will be overcrowded, and the world of 2050 will be one vast, jammed city. That 1999 isn't far off! It is almost a tomorrow, with many Kiwanians of today destined to be there. They therefore face a new adjustment, a new opportunity for humanitarian service.

Kiwanis has not been indifferent to all this. For one thing, the International officers years ago realized that "the old homestead" had been outgrown, and so in 1952 they began seeking a larger house for the headquarters family. Headquarters had been rented ones in a Chicago skyscraper; now we must find a place of our own.

Naturally, many cities begged to be hosts—New York, San Francisco, Miami, Houston, Phoenix, Denver, others, and any would have made an excellent setting. But the International Trustees did the right thing; they calmly repeated the truth, that Chicago is established as the Kiwanis home, is centrally located for the two founding nations. Then they bought an old mansion, the Blaine home at Rush and Erie Streets, after two years searching. It was a bargain. The Blaine house was razed, and with an initial fund of $1,000,000 already in hand, construction was begun in 1958. Thus on March 20, 1959, chairs, desks, records in filing cabinets, and personnel, moved from the old offices at 520 North Michigan Avenue, to beautiful new ones in a striking building at 101 East Erie Street.

Kiwanians from around the world now go to "One-Oh-One" with pride and pleasure. They get the red-carpet treatment. A beautiful girl greets them with smiles and dignity, a guide is provided, and a tour is enjoyed. On departure, the traveler gets a certificate of his call and other little souvenirs —good for a "make up" at his home club.

As of now, nobody can say how long One-Oh-One will serve. With population growing, with Kiwanis membership expanding, it too may soon be too small, out of date. New computers, new data processes, new mailing methods (all air mail as of now is obsolete; facsimile reproduction and delivery within 30 minutes is the coming thing, and soon!) will necessitate constant change. It may be that the year 2000 will see one central office in Chicago, with sky-scraper branches of Headquarters in New York, San Francisco, Houston, Phoenix, Denver, Frankfurt, Tokyo, Rio, Ciudad Mexico, Rome, Paris, London *et al.*

If such a one-world situation *is* coming, you can bet that Kiwanis will be on the job to help make it a magnificent place to live.

CHAPTER FOURTEEN

GOLDEN ANNIVERSARY

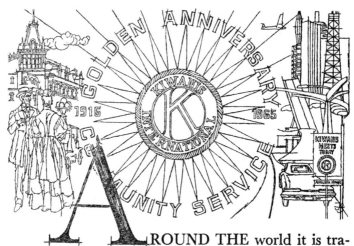

ROUND THE world it is traditional that whenever Mom and Pop have been married fifty years, all the children, grandchildren and friends gather to help them celebrate. And well they should. Simply to stay *alive* for half a century is a major achievement; alive and married to the same person, presumably with happiness, is miraculous indeed. Thus the people gather, re-live the past and re-dedicate for the future.

It was so with Kiwanis.

Its "Day" was January 21, 1965; the marriage had been consummated early in 1915, despite the hardships and horrors of a World War.

The groom? He was a handful of men in Detroit, Michigan; fellows as eager and unsure of themselves yet as determined as any bridegroom ever was. The bride? Ah, she was a delicate thing, yes! A genuine beauty, somewhat elusive, but eminently desirable. Her groom may have suspected that she would also be hard to control; that she would often confuse and frustrate him, yet would work marvels with and through him. She was, of course, the inspiriting new service club ideal—the selfless *Building* of betterment for mankind, the grand live-and-HELP-live attitude.

That marriage jelled, the loyalty endured, the "family" grew. And so it was meet and proper that in 1965 all the members should celebrate fifty years of compatibility, and that North America as a whole should drop by with good wishes and congratulations. There was food and fun and fanfare, pride was high yet humble. There was solemn recapitulation and re-assessment of values which lasted all through 1965, during which the marriage "vows" were spoken with fervor again. Happiness soared high. For unlike the literal Mom and Dad, *this* couple need have no fear of aging. The older it gets, the younger and more successful it becomes!

Even if you are an outsider it is fascinating to watch a family stage a celebration. This Golden Anniversary of Kiwanis became one of those quietly exciting and comforting years that sometimes comes to a nation. The people of every state soon sensed that, headlines and scary newscasts to the contrary notwithstanding, there was a *good* something extant in the land. Men and women of high stature were in charge of this country; not the "kooks" and crooks and screwball extremists that seemed to swarm out from under rocks.

This reassurance came at precisely the moment

when America needed it. The nation had been beset by many woes; war in Vietnam, strikes and "marches" and racial tensions, rebellious youths and aggressive communists, inflated costs and deflated dollars, even an unnecessarily bitter national election. All such horrors get publicity beyond their deserving. So then, Kiwanis on its Golden Anniversary rendered perhaps its greatest service to date—it devoted a year to reminding America, Canada and the world at large that God is *not* dead; that decency and honor, unselfishness and loyalty are by no means outmoded but have undergirded our society for many decades in a way that no force on earth can destroy. Such was the grandeur of the Celebration.

*   *   *

Formal "kick-off" for anniversary year observance was the publication in January 1965 of *The Kiwanis Magazine's* finest issue.

It was instantly eye appealing. Front cover showed "The Town"—the prototype Town in the U.S.A. as of 1915. It might be in Maine or Michigan or Mississippi or Montana or in any of a hundred other areas, for there was a sameness in small towns then, a seeming stability and immunity to change. Its name might have been Grass Roots, and its face—but let the magazine itself present it:

> The town grew from the river. Its earliest commerce was water borne, its local traffic horse-drawn even after the railroad came. In 1915, the automobile, no longer a novelty, had not yet supplanted the delivery wagon. Farmers still came in by horse and buggy over rutted country roads. The livery stable and the hitching rack served this era as the garage and the parking meter would serve another. Prosperous citizens had long since left the river, and Front

Street in 1915 was regarded as the tough part of town. The first railroad entered the town from the north, through the valley formed by the river. As the town resumed its growth around the station, a second line was built. Rail traffic boomed, and the railroad station became known officially as "Union Station"— though, to the motley crew of train-watchers gathered to watch the iron monsters rumble in, it was still "the depot."

The courthouse was built in the nineties, and "Courthouse Square" became the heart of the town. Main Street led from the depot to the square. Commerce Street and Bridge Street entered the square from the south. Old St. Paul's and the First Baptist Church were southwest of the square, in the heart of what was once the old residential area. Now the section to the north and east of the square had become the fashionable part of town, and Elmwood Drive "the place to live." The new high school was on the east side of town. The Polytechnic Institute of higher education had been built in the farmlands to the north of town at the crest of the benchland known as "Clanton Heights." The tannery was at the bend of the river, as was the foundry, shoe factory, wagon works, brickyard, and various other small industries. The tallest thing in town was the courthouse dome; but the new Franklin Block was five stories high and the old Grand Hotel was adding two extra floors.

Commerce Street, Bridge Street, Main Street and the Courthouse Square were paved with wooden blocks, but most streets were of dirt or gravel. Street cars ran on the main streets and out to the factory section along the river. Clay Center Road wound up the hill south of the river. The Road was a favorite challenge to men like "Dutch" Meyer, who owned one of the first automobiles in the town. For years "Dutch" held the record for driving up that hill before having to shift into "low." In the winter and spring, no one would even attempt that hill without chains—and sometimes the chains failed. Farmers living along Clay Center Road were used to harnessing a team of horses to rescue the motorist who couldn't make it under his own power. "Zeke" Porterfield used to claim he made half his livestock-feed money that way.

An event of lasting importance took place in a

dim-lit, cluttered office on the rim of "The Bend," in the south part of town. There, on a bitter cold January night in 1918, Jack Fletcher, owner of the Fletcher Wagon Works, got together with his friends Homer Smith, "Si" Sherman, and "Dutch" Meyer, and formed the town's first Kiwanis Club.

At charter night ceremonies on April 29, 1918, Jack, who had been unanimously elected president of the new club, made an important announcement to the assembled civic leaders. Kiwanis, he informed them, was not going to become just another fellowship-and-chowder group. Kiwanis, he continued, had an ideal of service. And to convince his listeners of his sincerity, he then ticked off three specific ways in which the new group meant to be of immediate service to its community. Jack promised first, that the club would participate 100 per cent in the Liberty Bond Drive; second, that it would assist in the preparation of vacant lots for Victory Gardens; and finally, that it would pledge full support for the proposed Chamber of Commerce Building.

It was an auspicious beginning; and Kiwanis effort did not flag as time passed. Sponsorship of Boy Scout troops, better road campaigns, banquets feting the local football team, and efforts to improve relationships with the surrounding farm community, were the order of the day in post World War I years. Within its first five years, membership doubled; and under the leadership of the legendary Judge Amos Scroggs, of Spanish-American War fame, Kiwanis began making an impressive name for itself in the town and in the neighboring countryside. Civic leaders gravitated to it, one by one, in the sure knowledge that its membership could be called upon to respond to any community need.

The club's first big challenge came in 1924. The thin soil of the hill farms to the north of the town had worn out. The fields were eroded, and most of the farms were idle or deserted. Title for much of the land was held by local banks; and when Willard Ayers, president of the Commercial Bank, proposed to fellow Kiwanians that they set up a Boy Scout camp in Funks Grove, they responded with enthusiasm, within a short period raising enough money for an equity, and for organized crews to build cabins. With this nucleus, additional land was acquired over the years and planted with trees. Today what had been a gullied, barren eyesore is a wooded hillside of several hundred acres.

The Polytechnic Institute was suffering in the late twenties. Originally endowed by private philanthropies in the East, it had drawn on rural areas for its student body; but with the death of the original benefactors and the gradual attrition of endowment, plans had been completed to abandon the school. The Kiwanis club by itself could not save Polytechnic; but the club could and did spearhead a drive to raise an educational and building fund that tided the institution over the crisis, and provided the foundation for what in 1965 was to be known as the Junior College. The man who did most to get this drive underway was the dynamic young lawyer, Frank Crenshaw, whose grandfather was a local pioneer.

The south and east sides of town were steadily deteriorating in the twenties. The Kiwanis club helped establish parks and playgrounds in a few abandoned lots; but it was not until the early thirties that many of the shacks along Front Street were torn down and residents began shoring up the old waterfront piers for pleasure boat use. Little more could be done, however, because the town was then in the midst of the Great Depression. The tannery and the shoe factory had closed down. The wagon works had long since failed, and no new industries had replaced the ones that were lost. But although the Kiwanis club lost manpower, it did not lose its sense of responsibility to the community. Under square-jawed Fred Keith, who later became district governor, its members provided leadership for a campaign that started construction of the town's first airport, west of the river—an airport now easily accessible by way of the four-lane bridge that had been built in the twenties. With this beginning came the drive to make the town more attractive to new industry. Rail and air facilities were excellent. By the late thirties the town was ready for the war boom that was to come.

Although the town was growing rapidly to the north and the east, the downtown business section spreading out from Courthouse Square was still the center of trade. New schools had been built in the outlying areas, and a new high school east of the town in the early twenties. Residents in the north section were proposing a bond issue for a high school to serve their area. Kiwanis of course lost members to the armed forces in the war years; but the club was growing, acquiring new members from new businesses and the new industries geared to the war effort. During the war, Kiwanis helped establish and maintain a local service center, provided leadership for scrap drives, and for various other home front activities.

The high school proposed for the north section of the town prior to the war was built in the post-war years. In 1951, local Kiwanians sponsored the first Key Club in East High School; and when a second downtown Kiwanis club was built in 1953, the members of that club—led by Frank Crenshaw II—sponsored a Key Club in North High School shortly thereafter.

New multiple-story buildings were shooting up like dandelions in the downtown section. Courthouse Square was now the frequent setting for full-dress traffic jams. The old courthouse could no longer accommodate the city's numerous departmental functions. Space was being rented wherever possible in nearby office buldings. In 1955 a new civic center was built; and on its completion, the old courthouse was torn down and a traffic circle engineered and built around an imposing war memorial. The downtown section had been losing business to outlying shopping areas and this rejuvenation of the central section halted somewhat the trend toward the suburbs—although Clanton Heights was now entirely residential, and a new suburban area with its own Kiwanis club had grown up in the river valley north of the town.

The old Polytechnic Institute (now the Junior College) had grown through endowments, educational bonds, and state aid until it was a flourishing institution with a small campus and stadium. Key Clubs in North and East High Schools had found much to do in providing leadership services for their schools. The initial grading and preparation of the parking lot adjacent to the athletic field of East High School was done by the Key Club of that school, with the help of members of the sponsoring Kiwanis group.

Memorial Hospital at the foot of Clanton Heights

was considered the edge of town in 1915. A modest but adequate building at that time, in 1965 it had been enlarged to meet local needs. The Kiwanis Wing, established in 1928 as a tangible memorial to the club's tenth-anniversary celebration, was now a well-equipped and staffed center of research for treatment of spastic paralysis. Over the years, other Kiwanians had raised money for their various community projects in various ways. One noteworthy continuing project was sponsorship of community concerts. When North High School was built, the two downtown Kiwanis clubs joined forces to sponsor these concerts, as well as a travelogue series held in the auditorium of that High School.

In the suburban area to the north, Kiwanis and various other civic groups had been meeting in school rooms and church basements. In 1961 a new community center was dedicated. The man who laid the cornerstone was Eddie Porterfield, past president of the north club and grandson of Zeke Porterfield, who used to haul "gas buggies" out of the mire of Clay Center Road. This new building was overdue; for, in addition to the new businesses that had moved to the town, there had sprung up in the old river front area a gigantic new industrial complex.

After an exhaustive study, the Intercontinental Chemical Corporation had selected the town, not only for its strategic location and rail and air facilities, but for its many cultural, educational, and residential advantages. The riverfront park and marina had been an important factor. Three years before, Kiwanis had joined with other civic groups in supporting the garden club's initial effort to develop a park along the banks of the river. Once started, the plans mushroomed; and by 1965 there was not only a marina, but also an extensive park, complete with picnic facilities and a band shell for summer concerts.

A new bridge had been built spanning the river to the west to accommodate the new highway, which was elevated above the railway yards before descending to street level. The Clay Center Road still winds up the hill on the south side of the river; but today, "Dutch" Meyers' record is smashed almost every second, while a Kiwanis road sign welcomes the automobile traveler as he approaches the town on the 4-lane highway. The land on the south side of the river is still farmland, with the exception of the television transmitter on the highest point of the hill. Lately there's been talk about putting a park on some of this land; the Kiwanis clubs have appointed a joint committee to consider it.

In those simple, forceful and quietly dramatic words was the fifty-year history of a legendary Kiwanis Town in the United States portrayed. Almost any Kiwanian could envision it as his own home town. But to help him, there was a gatefold cover for the magazine. Front showed The Town in full color, as of 1915; The innerfold showed it in full color as of 1965.

Thus did the official organ of Kiwanis present the changing face of America during the early half of this century, then in its text show the great growing heart of the nation. This issue of the magazine had 100 pages, and showed that Kiwanis at that time had grown from its humble start in Detroit, all the way across the U.S.A. and Canada and into foreign lands.

In that issue Ted R. Johnson, an International Trustee, in an editorial said, "This year we will be casting many a glance backward to 'the good old days.' May I suggest that some of these glances be made to prepare us for the future." Ted of course was delicately setting the mood for the whole Anniversary Celebration. He was saying, wisely, that history is of no value except as a guide for improvement. International President Edward B. Moylan, Jr., echoed and expanded these sentiments, and one way or another so did every other Kiwanis leader.

Yet this issue of *The Kiwanis Magazine* was not all serious. Pages of cartoons depicted typical Kiwanis song leaders, in high fun. Even more hilarious were pictures of that magnificent creation which started as a plaything of the rich then stayed to change the whole North American way of life—the horseless carriage. Included were a "Tin Lizzie" Ford, a Chevrolet coupe (America never did quite decide whether to call it "koop" or "koo-pay") and other makes. Each required you to climb two or more high steps to get in the "tonneau," and you were protected from rain—call it protection—by a flexible combination of oil cloth and isinglass. Thus nostalgia assailed every reader over forty years of age. The motor car and Kiwanis were kids together and grew up together.

All told, that issue of *The Kiwanis Magazine* became a beautiful, permanent souvenir showing incidents and ideals from the past, then upgrading the aims and idealism for the future. The issue for the year 2015 will have to strain to make itself a better one.

* * *

Soon after the magazine appeared, clubs everywhere launched the great Golden Anniversary celebration. Mechanics of the party one way or another touched almost every citizen. These community leaders who comprise Kiwanis are experts at "putting something across." Backstage preparations had started two years ahead, with brainstorming sessions in District Offices and especially at International Headquarters in Chicago. By mid-1964 the master plan was complete, and by September copies were in the hands of every club president. Each club was instructed to do its own thinking, work in its own manner to fit its individual community. But here, gentlemen, is a kit of helpful hints and suggestions which you are free to use if you wish.

The purpose of the observance was clearly stated at the top of Page 1:

> To provide Kiwanians with a "platform" from which the Kiwanis story can be told dramatically to the general public, and thus assure renewed acceptance of the Kiwanis program.

This did not mean simply a heavy promotion to increase the size of the organization. Key words there are "the Kiwanis story." The Kiwanis story—worth repeating endlessly—is that the only tenable guide to successful living is helping one another; is building the human spirit, body and mind. Acceptance of such an ideal can become a contagion. That's what the Kiwanians wanted, that was the core of their whole Anniversary effort. It was "publicity," yes; but for a way of life, one without selfish gain.

Another important piece of printed matter issued from Chicago was *Ten Kiwanis Objectives For The Golden Anniversary Year*. This three-color folder stressed all the major areas of Kiwanis concern, backing up the official administrative theme for 1965—"Community Service—We Build." Ten statements gave all Kiwanians a concise sense of direction in explaining the organization's purpose. Hundreds of thousands of these were distributed.

Later in the year a special pictorial synopsis of Kiwanis history was ready for distribution. It showed activities from 1915 to 1965, and became another treasured item. It was titled *Kiwanis At Fifty*. And, again, readers have wondered what better portrayal might be dreamed up for the forthcoming *Kiwanis At One Hundred.* A scientist, speaking in Houston, answered them. He said, "You may not need any sort of printed matter then. Your headquarters probably will simply issue "Item Number Nine, Thought Transference!" Which is a little bit frightening, because it may well be true!

As at any Golden Anniversary "wedding" observance, festivity and food had honored places among Kiwanians that year. First big banquet was in Cobo Hall in Detroit. There the Number 1 Club of Kiwanis, with the Michigan Kiwanis District and the Kiwanis Board of International Trustees, gathered in what the newspapers called solemn conclave. National, state and local dignitaries outside the organization were present as well wishers, and incidentally went away deeply impressed. Actual program dramatized Kiwanis' founding, paid tribute to those Detroit men responsible for Kiwanis and its growth. A new Kiwanis International film had its premiere, then was released for all North America to enjoy via club, television and private showings.

Pretty soon people could sense the groundswell of interest, coast to coast. News media anounced that the Kiwanis International Convention in New York City July 4-6, 1965, would be a Golden Anniversary celebration, and that a day at the New York World's Fair would be devoted to Kiwanis.

Thus new-generation folk began asking, "What *is* Kiwanis? What's it all about?"

That was exactly what the members wanted; stimulate the questions, then provide the answers.

"Ours is not a 'closed corporation,'" the organization quietly replied. "Membership is restricted to the willing, the capable leaders. But our goals are for the upgrading of every human life on earth."

Members broke all records swarming to that Convention in New York. Each got a special Golden Anniversary Souvenir Program, a keepsake. All were awed by the magnitude of Kiwanis achievement as reviewed there, and more so by plans for the second fifty years.

At that Convention, and in that same month across the continent, Kiwanians re-enacted or re-told the very first project of the very first Kiwanis club, No. 1 in Detroit. This was the literal adoption of a young boy from a broken home. His last name was officially changed to Kiwanis, so that Walter Kiwanis was brought up and educated by members of that club. Since then other clubs have officially or otherwise "adopted" unfortunate youths, following Detroit's fine precedent.

The real heart of the Golden Anniversary observance was the presentation of Blank Checks of Service by clubs to the mayors of their communities. Many districts presented similar checks to their state governors or provincial premiers. Each check pledged the club to contribute goods or services to the community as a "birthday gift in reverse," a tangible "thank you" for the privilege of serving throughout the life of the club. The total value of such things as parks built or refurbished, clinics constructed or provided, and services rendered in hundreds of different ways, was staggering . . up into the scores of millions of dollars; the goodwill these checks produced was priceless.

The continental publicity push began to snowball by March of 1965. A beautiful bronze pocket piece the size of a half dollar was struck for distribution at International headquarters—reminder for any carrier that he is a chosen man, set apart, for having accepted the highest possible idealism. Many exquisite pamphlets and other printed helps streamed from the offices at 101 East Erie Street, Chicago. Then as the year progressed, people everywhere began to see "the service story" proclaimed on massive billboards, on theater screens, on television, in daily and weekly newspapers, and in magazines. Radio voices dramatized the achievements of Kiwanians, both locally and around the world. Window cards, car stickers, posters on store windows, all did their bit. Kiwaniannes were especially active in this work, for they could devote time to it that their husbands often could ill spare, and their enthusiasm was no less high.

The ladies of Kiwanis also were cooperative in staging "History Nights," social affairs on or near January 21 with Golden Anniversary themes, held in hundreds of towns. Typically, the people came to these parties clad in costumes of 1915—and before you laugh, consider how your *present* clothing is going to look to your grandchildren in the year 2015! It was great fun, and the people, including the oldsters, were full of prance. In most cases the party orchestras, also in period dress, played nostalgic music. The group singing was memorable, with men and women belting out such ageless numbers as *Alexander's Ragtime Band* which, come to think of it, has endured almost as well as Kiwanis itself, even though many persons considered it slightly sinful when the fellows sang it back in World War I years.

Altogether, then, the Golden Anniversary parties were unforgettable. "The wedding" had endured, the family had grown immeasurably, the prosperity was high.

*   *   *

Because Golden means Fiftieth, Kiwanians in the U.S.A. and Canada tied to the "fifty" theme, with hundreds of clubs in 1965 setting themselves very special goals—

Fifty pieces of equipment to be furnished this year for Boys' Clubs, Boy Scout Troops, Girls' Clubs, playgrounds and such.

Fifty boys and girls helped to find needed jobs part or full time.

Science Fairs for youth, showing fifty ways in which the former drudgeries and inconveniences of daily living had been supplanted by modern scientific progress.

Work with local newspapers, radio and television stations to select the town "Teen of the week" — based on citizenship excellence — for fifty consecutive weeks.

Fifty books and fifty magazine subscriptions sent by the club to underdeveloped nations, to spread the ideals of Americanism.

Fifty pounds of clothing per month sent to one or more needy missions, nations or areas in America or abroad.

Arranging for members of Kiwanis to hold at least fifty civic posts (with or without pay) in the local community.

A distinguished local senior citizen honored each week for fifty weeks.

Outstanding minister, priest or rabbi, or layman church member, honored each week for fifty weeks.

Fifty hymnals or Bibles presented to a church.

Fifty sermons taped in church then distributed for use by shut-ins at hospitals and at home.

Fifty mentally retarded youths guaranteed a week or more in camp.

The list might go on for pages because clubmen began to make a project of dreaming up "fifties" projects! Some of course became quite bizarre—in west Texas, for instance, a group set out to kill fifty rattlesnakes during the year. They killed fourteen— all they could find. Alibi was that Congress had ruled rattlers subversive and President Johnson—who once saw a small one on his ranch—turned the F.B.I. out after them. Republicans in the club protested, but nothing came of it. Then Reps and Demos alike assembled to make fifty calls on kids in an orphans' home, carrying toys and other goodies.

This Golden Anniversary opened endless new ideas for program committees. Headquarters in Chicago supplied helpful guidance also. Net result was a series of extra-good meetings all over the Kiwanis world. Typically, a *Parade of Leaders* was staged by hundreds of clubs.

"Expression of appreciation," one district governor explained, "is the finest but most neglected of the gentle arts. Every man of whatever status needs to be appreciated, needs to know he is important at least in some small degree. This is an urge in him more powerful than the craving for sex, food, success or any other, and the modern psychologists verify it. Thus we can *Build* the human spirit admirably in this kind of service."

The Parades therefore honored many men and women who have been outstanding in Kiwanis work on the local scenes. Programs were based somewhat on the big one used for similar expressions of appreciation at the International Convention in New York. Similar format was used in the district conventions for 1965. Past and incumbent officers, and their wives, were honored, and one of the governors gave dramatic testimonial in turn. He said that he had taken office rather hurriedly, then discovered that he lacked the know-how for it, felt insecure and ineffectual as a district leader. Then as a husband will, he told his wife about it.

"Let me read you a clipping that I have saved," said she, gently. "A thing from President Coolidge. I clipped it from the *Gong and Gavel* page in *The Kiwanis Magazine*. It goes like this:

"Nothing in the world can take the place of persistence. Talent will not—nothing is more common than unsuccessful men with talent. Genius will not—unrewarded genius is almost a proverb. Education will not—the world is full of educated derelicts. Persistence and determination alone are omnipotent."

That governor went back to his duties and saw them through with such devotion that he inspired every club he contacted. The result was a banner year for his district.

He was governor in an eastern district, but the reach for excellence was not limited to any area.

Harken now to excerpts from a Golden Anniversary speech by Lawrence Mehren, past lieutenant governor of the Southwest District:

"What motivated Albert Schweitzer, and all others of his kind? The answer is that early in his career he based his philosophy on what he called 'reverence for life,' and on a deep feeling of obligation to serve his fellow man in thought and action.

"In the heart of every one of us exists that inescapable feeling of obligation to help others. This haunting thing is the driving force behind the United Funds, the Boy Scouts, Y.M.C.A., Christmas Seals, and, yes, all service clubs. These are the *manifestations* of the yearnings to help. They are the magic keys to happiness.

"In Chicago on a bitterly cold day, a Kiwanian paused to help a small boy who had lost the dollar given him to buy groceries. The lad was crying, saying that his dad would beat him, as he often did. Of course the Kiwanian supplied another dollar, and the lad, waving goodbye, tearfully said, 'Gee, mister, I wish *you* was my daddy.'

"Could a million dollars have brought that man greater satisfaction?

"The need today is for men who will pray, 'God, let me be aware of the pain that comes to others because of heartache. God, let me be aware of their hunger and hopelessness. And then, dear God, let me do something to alleviate the heartache and hunger and hopelessness of these souls.'

"Another man, an American soldier in London, asked a little ragamuffin what he wanted for Christmas. 'Please sir,' begged the boy, 'I want to be loved.'

"It was a cry in the wilderness, heard hourly by us all. The craving for an end to heartache, the abject yearning for love—simple, ordinary, marvelous, miracle-working love—is heard at our doorsteps and around the world. *In this lies the greatest opportunity for Kiwanis.* We accepted it for our first fifty years. We must open our doors to it even wider now. Keep in mind, gentlemen, that Kiwanis is not merely something you join; it is something you *do.*"

It is significant that such an inspired talk came not from a preacher but from a high-level business executive. Small wonder he was honored by his fellow Kiwanians at Anniversary time.

In the 1965 District Conventions, and especially in the individual club meetings that year, honoring of leaders became an inspiration for all listeners. Invariably the mood was one of maturity and sincerity, not of boredom or frivolity. Even sometimes cynical newspaper reporters would come away touched, inspired.

"Gentlemen," the speaker of the moment would say, "there is no lonelier estate than to lead; no more demanding responsibility than to know that in the final reckoning, you, and you alone, must make the decisions upon which others may stand or fall. Hence it is our privilege to honor those who have contributed so much, voluntarily, without whom neither this club, this district, nor Kiwanis International could have lived, and grown, and become a mighty force for good."

These are serious words, earnest words—and let the cynics beware. Let the pseudo-sophisticated citizenry call such speechmakers "old fashioned" or "corny" or "square." These phonies tried such ridicule shortly after Kiwanis and sister service clubs were founded, predicting that the clubs would strangle in their own sentimental idealism.

But the clubs survived, matured, became world powerful. The generation of phonies is long since buried, just as any new generation of them inevitably will be.

CHAPTER FIFTEEN

THE FABULOUS SIXTIES

LONG ABOUT the year 2000 some scholarly historian is going to write that the 1960's seemed to be the decade when America and Canada shifted gears.

The nations started off crawling in "low," which was natural. They shifted to "second" somewhere about 1915—the year Kiwanis was founded—then stepped on the gas. Acceleration was noticed right along, so that when mid-century turned, both countries were roaring with power and speed. Then suddenly in the 1960's we seemed to shift—automatically this time, without conscious effort—into "high." Net result was that more things were done, more accomplished from 1960 to 1966 than in any previous twenty years.

Economic and social analysts of the year 2000 will verify what their kind are already saying—that the speed-up has been due to a fantastic increase in human knowledge.

This truth was dramatized in the spring of 1966 in this fashion:

Envision three perpendicular lines on a graph.

All of human knowledge from the beginning of time to the beginning of the Steam Age is represented by the first line—six inches tall.

The additional human knowledge learning from the beginning of the Steam Age to the beginning of the Atomic Age is represented by the second line— eighteen inches tall.

The still additional knowledge learned by all of humanity from the beginning of the Atomic Age down to 1966—now brace yourself—is represented by the third line, *which would have to be taller than the Washington Monument!*

This shocker is almost unbelievable. Yet as you look around, observing what's being done (moon photos, walking in space, supersonic planes, "super-human" computers etc.) you realize that this is little if any exaggeration. Science alone can verify it, for we are told that 80 percent of all the scientists who ever lived on earth are alive today!

This, the seventh edition of *The Widening Path,* truly is being published in the middle of a fabulous era. The middle? More likely the mere beginning, for those same astute scholars and analysts say that the third graph line is still shooting upward like the mercury in a thermometer suddenly plunged into hot water. By 1980 it may be as high as Mount Everest.

Quite naturally, the men and women of Kiwanis pause here to ask, "What is our service club's position in this fabulous growth?"

There can be no sharply defined answer. Nobody can say precisely where the world is going, and no experts, not even at International Headquarters in Chicago, can say exactly how Kiwanis will fit in. But one fact is absolutely certain—Kiwanians *will* be there, will continue to gain in numbers and prestige, will continue to be leaders in the upper five percent of the citizens who run America and Canada, and by a rapid extension, the rest of the free world. Awareness of this destiny is an exhilaration.

Many reactions have been heard to this growth talk from the leaders in Kiwanis. For instance, these gems, gleaned from a thousand or more speeches by District Governors, Lieutenant-Governors, club presidents, and just substantial ordinary-Joe members:

"It is correct to say that Kiwanis has done good things during its first half century. Yet they are negligible compared to what we are going to do. With sister service groups, *in the next thirty years we shall re-build America.* We shall give it a grandeur beyond anything the founding fathers ever dreamed, or that we ourselves can now envision."

What powerful words of confidence!

"Many people in this era act fearful. They are afraid of the Russians, for example. Every so often the United States and the Soviet Union are presented as being economic equals, but they aren't. Here is what the U.S.A. would have to do to get equal with the U.S.S.R.:

1. Abandon three-fifths of our steel capacity.
2. Abandon two-thirds of our petroleum production.

3. Scrap two out of three of our hydro-electric plants.
4. Forget more than 90 percent of our natural gas reserves.
5. Eliminate 95 percent of our electric motor output.
6. Rip up 14 of every 15 miles of paved highways.
7. Destroy 2 of every 3 miles of railroads.
8. Sink eight of every nine of our ocean-going ships.
9. Junk 19 of every 20 of our cars and trucks.
10. Transfer 60 million Americans back to the farms.
11. Destroy 40 million television sets.
12. Rip out nine of every 10 telephones."

Again, an upbeat; a positive note of appreciation, not of defeatism and fear. That speaker was saying that we may not now know all the answers, but we have demonstrated an ability to go out and find them, we are undergirded with physical and mental muscles of steel.

Or look now at this third approach to the matter of speed, human knowledge and philosophy:

"We have come to a time of re-appraisal. We are asking ourselves anew, 'Exactly what is happiness, what is success?' And the answers are coming through clearly. To achieve a successful life, you have to be as wonderfully 'corny,' unsophisticated and genuine as Lawrence Welk music. You have to reconsider that almost-forgotten Biblical injunction to be as a child, simple, naive, trusting, even while remaining wary and strong. Come to think of it, what other tenable standard have we to go by? Madison Avenue and the publicity boys? Pornography Magazine? The Pentagon? *What's wrong with the Holy Bible as a guide for living?"*

That roaring indictment came not from a Billy Graham or equal, not from a fence-straddling politician, but from a very typical grass roots Kiwanian who is president of a bank.

"God has given us a world," a fourth man echoed him, "that nothing but our own folly keeps from being a paradise. The moment in history has come when we are realizing our folly and setting out to correct it. This will take less time than most men think."

Hence it is probable that the historian in the year 2000 will record the fabulous 1960's as the decade of renewed idealism; this despite all the horrors of the time. Kiwanis has always been based on applied idealism—but this does not mean that its members have floated along with their heads in the clouds. They have been idealists in the sense that George Washington, Abraham Lincoln and Theodore Roosevelt were, dreamers who were realists as well. It is never easy to "Build;" sometimes literal bloodshed is required, and almost always snipers are shooting at you. For example, back there when Kiwanis and other great service organizations were very young, some of the so-called *literati* of America discovered them and, with incredible presumption, set out to make them objects of scorn.

It began in the early 1920's. College youth, "freed" in its thinking by World War I, was worshiping at the glittering shrines of George Jean

Nathan and H. L. Mencken—and being called flappers and jellybeans for it. Cynicism was flaunted by our "brilliant" citizens, and several Sinclair Lewises, including Sinclair Lewis in the flesh, arose as writing opportunists to take advantage of it. Altogether these picturesque folk made quite a deal of noise. They told us—with a lofty sympathy, to be sure—that such unsophisticated organizations as Kiwanis were mushroom growths that would soon disappear in the national upsurge of realism. We have already seen what happened; the cynics are dead (replaced by a new and equally impotent set) but the clubs are multi-million strong. This survival of the clubs was a God-given thing; America *might* have gone to the dogs back there, to the cynics and pseudo-sophisticates such as wrecked ancient Greece and Rome, because our early club meetings were no great shakes. But the meetings improved rapidly, and the idealism was applied with increasing fervor, first across the United States, then across Canada, and finally into foreign lands.

The sixties will always be "fabulous" to Kiwanians because in this decade they did lengthen their outreach. Almost from the beginning (January 1915) many men felt that the service organization should be spread into other lands. It was natural, therefore, for a new club to be set up in Hamilton, Ontario, in 1916.

But other devout leaders were still influenced by North American isolationism. We vaguely distrusted "foreigners," forgetting that Latins and Germans and English and Asiatics were all cast from the same divine mold "in His own image." We had been at-

[169]

tacked by the Kaiser, but we were not invaded so we fervently shouted "Thank God for the Atlantic Ocean," never dreaming that it soon was to become a pond over which friends or enemies could jump almost at will. We went Over There, won a war and came back; Over Here, we felt isolated, secure, apart. Then of course all that changed. Wendell Willkie tried to tell us we were one world, but we were slow to accept it.

Kiwanis, which has always reacted to the challenges of the times—but never without due consideration—saw that its own idealism applied to the new and shrunken world.

It was on April 17, 1962 that Kiwanis first "went abroad." The first club outside the United States and Canada was literally in sight of southern California . . in Tijuana, Baja California, Republic of Mexico.

This was the first step in international extension, the first of many which came, and are coming today, with ever increasing volume and rapidity.

It came following action of delegates to the international convention in Toronto in 1961 who adopted a resolution reading, "We favor the establishment of Kiwanis clubs in other countries in addition to Canada and the United States, under the safeguards fixed by the Board of Trustees of Kiwanis International."

Actually, the preparations had been under way for several years. There had been a Special International Committee on Foreign Extension to study the problems. It was replaced by a committee from the International Board of Trustees, which set up plans leading to approval of the move. A highly detailed procedure was necessitated, but in brief it was as follows:

1. Clubs would be organized only in nations which permit to individuals freedom of assembly, expression and action.
2. They would be assisted in their organization by existing clubs in the United States and Canada, and would be attached to the districts in which those clubs were located until enough clubs were formed outside the U.S. and Canada to permit formation of additional districts.
3. Clubs would be encouraged to engage in activities in support of the "way of life of free men." All activities of such clubs would be entirely compatible with the Objects of Kiwanis International.

Thus the Tijuana club came into being forty-seven years after Kiwanis itself did. It was sponsored by two good neighbors, the clubs of San Diego and Chula Vista, California. About sixty charter members made up that first "foreign" club. Benjamin Garcia, a race course official, was elected its first *presidente,* and he officiated with all the grace, courtesy and tact that any leader ever showed.

At that historic moment, I. R. Witthuhn, the Kiwanis International president, said, "This is no spur-of-the-moment action on our part. Kiwanians have long been anxious to spread their concept of the service club and its ideals into lands other than the United States and Canada. Now the time is propitious. Clubs will be organized only in nations which permit to individuals freedom of assembly, expression and action, and will be encouraged to engage in activities supporting the way of free men."

From that moment, things began to hum. New Kiwanis Clubs were chartered in Mexico City, Mexicali, Ensenada, Monterrey, Guadalajara. Nassau, Bahamas, joined the clan. Then in February 1963, Kiwanis officially jumped the Atlantic and appeared in Vienna, Austria, with official charter date following on May 4—another historic moment. Big Names from the United States were at Vienna, and the actual ceremonies were of such nature as to be emotionally moving, a significant hands-across-the-sea proclamation of friendship and agreement to serve mankind together.

Before January 1, 1966, the following countries had Kiwanis clubs: United States, Canada, Mexico, Bahamas, Austria, Switzerland, Belgium, Germany, Norway, Iceland, Japan (Tokyo got the first club in Asia) Jamaica, Philippines, Netherlands Antilles, Puerto Rico, France, Holland, forty-three of them outside the U.S. and Canada. By July 1, 1966, twelve more foreign clubs had been organized.

All European clubs sent delegates to a conference in Vienna on May 21-22, 1966. This was primarily a training session—and looked much like a meeting of United Nations. The group also considered advances made to date on the formation of a European Federation of Kiwanis Clubs.

As with clubs in North America, activities of the foreign groups cover a wide range of community interest. One club operates a cancer clinic. Vienna, first in Europe, has a project in which youngsters design and fabricate tile mosaics, which are sold to schools and public buildings for display, the proceeds going to youth charities.

The Oslo, Norway, Kiwanians "adopted" 150 girls and boys in a school for mentally retarded children, giving them the "important experiences normal children have during their formative years in a normal family environment." The men have set up theatrical performances for the children, have taken them on boat trips on the Oslo fjord, and to soccer matches. A pre-Christmas dinner was arranged for them. A spokesman for this club said, "The state can provide food, clothing and shelter for these boys and girls, but Kiwanians are providing love." Kiwanis Clubs everywhere may well take note!

The club in Tijuana transports crippled children to a hospital in nearby San Diego "for examination and curation"—and if the English translation by them isn't perfect, the meaningful heart interest is. This club also provided 1300 bags of food, 23,000 bags of candies and 15,000 toys for poor people of Tijuana at Christmas. But its most important project is the operation of a Cancer Detection Clinic which, at this writing, had examined nearly 1,000 women and provided treatment where this was needed and feasible.

In Zurich, Switzerland, as a Golden Anniversary project in 1965, Kiwanians held a bazaar for the benefit of children in a home for the mentally retarded. Proceeds were about $10,000. This club also has rebuilt an old house into suitable quarters for a youth home. At Christmas it too provided toys, skis, clothing, candles, bed linen, woolen blankets and such to thirty needy families.

In nearby Basel, Kiwanians regularly invite overseas students attending Basel University into their homes for dinner and "a taste of home life and hospitality," and they run a car service to take cerebral palsied youngsters to school.

There are an increasing number of such projects in the foreign towns, and if they have the "flavor" of those which have been the hallmark of Kiwanis service in the United States and Canada for more than fifty years, it is not by accident. The Kiwanis spirit of service is just as appropriate in Kamchatka as in Kalamazoo; just as wanted and gratifying in overseas clubs and cities as in English, French and Spanish speaking North America. One of the members of that first Asiatic club, in Tokyo, made a little off-the-record speech to some of the guests from North America when his club was chartered. Through an interpreter he said, "If Germany, Italy and Japan had understood the American and Canadian ideals as Kiwanis activates them, there never would have been a World War II."

He may or may not have been correct, but at least he revealed the yearnings of decent men around the world, and pointed a finger for Kiwanis direction henceforth. As this edition of this book goes to press early in 1967, there are 58 Kiwanis Clubs in 18 countries outside the United States and Canada. Hundreds more will be appearing. The Sixties must be recorded as fabulous, yes; but the Seventies are almost sure to go down in history as the decade of Kiwanis' greatest worldwide expansion. Men of good will everywhere will take pride in this spread of a selfless ideal.

CHAPTER SIXTEEN

OUR SACRED NINETY MINUTES

O MATTER how wonderful the stated ideals, the philosophies, the operational plans and such, no service organization is going to function well without a constant, subtle "needling" of its members.

For Kiwanis this takes place once each week at what the men have begun to call "the sacred ninety minutes."

They refer to the club meeting itself. There is no law about it, but the usual time for these regular assemblies is an hour and a half. Some cut it ten minutes short; many don't hesitate to run two hours, especially at night. Originally referred to as "luncheon clubs," more of them now meet at sundown than at noon. This has some merit; the fellows can gather at 5:30 p.m., enjoy a dinner and program together, and still get home shortly after 7 o'clock, thus not taking important time away from either business or family. Many clubs have chosen the breakfast hour —7 a.m. assembly, then in the office before 9. It is a matter of choice, based on the convenience of the individual club's members. But the time is "sacred," even so.

Many of the early-day Kiwanis meetings suffered from poor programming and seemed to lack a sense of direction. Not until O. Sam Cummings, the first full-time International Secretary, began to needle the organization did Kiwanis clubs begin to achieve a uniformity and directional pattern.

But that was only the first step. The second was fostered by the man who succeeded Cummings as secretary—Fred C. W. Parker. He was destined to serve as International Secretary for twenty years. It was under his patient guidance that the subtler feeling of international outreach began to filter into all Kiwanians.

"This stemmed from the fact that men felt a strong sense of responsibility in conducting the individual weekly programs," Fred said in later years. "The club officers in almost every town have come to realize that their election was an honor only in so far as they furnish a leadership at once humble and strong."

Such idealism was characteristic of Secretary Parker. He saw, along with Roe Fulkerson and others during his time, that the real heart of Kiwanis is in the club meeting because of the fellowship created there. Under Fred Parker, Kiwanis made fellowship a vitalized word. Fred was made Secretary Emeritus in 1940 and given a retirement income, but lived to enjoy it for only five years. That was long enough for him to know that the younger man who succeeded him was doing an even better job. Kiwanis had reached out into another and, in some ways, more experienced organization to get its third executive leader. He was Oscar Ewald Peterson, an officer of the Young Men's Christian Association.

"Pete" Peterson had come originally from St. Paul and had been trained in personnel work with the United States Steel Corporation. Then in the more idealistic YMCA field he had developed remarkable insight into the character of men who made up the United States and Canada. And in the march of Kiwanis history, Pete Peterson "perfected" the individual club meeting.

He broadened the appeal of that sacred ninety minutes. He drove home the fact that it was *only* an hour and a half, so fellowship and inspiration must not be handicapped by mechanics which might better operate backstage anyway. Keep the meetings alive, said he; that way you can prove to the world that Kiwanis is a service organization rather than just a group of luncheon clubs.

In 1966 Pete put himself out to pasture, but colleagues and friends soon observed that he was still full of prance. He had seen Kiwanis move from early adolescence to maturity, indeed had guided those difficult years with skilled and kindly hand.

He was succeeded by two other "good men and true." One was Reginald P. Merridew, called "Reg." Officially on October 24, 1966, he became the Secretary of Kiwanis International. Prior to that date, on May 15, 1966, the second man was formally ap-

[177]

pointed Associate Secretary of Kiwanis International and, along with Reg, ex-officio member of the Board of Trustees. He was Lawrence A. Hapgood, called Larry.

Those two friends took their offices prayerfully. And well they should. Kiwanis was no longer a one-horse organization. In fact it was a heavy load for two horses, and the accelerating growth would soon require multi-powered teams. But there have to be leaders, and so — Reg and Larry, 1966. Good wishes and God-bless-yous poured in from all the Kiwanis nations. When the two friends took office in Chicago, they faced the responsibility of guiding 270,000 men in 5,400 Kiwanis clubs in 18 nations. They had a big, experienced staff at headquarters in Chicago to help them, they had wholehearted support from elected officers and Trustees. Confidence was never higher.

Rank and file Kiwanians might ask how the two top Kiwanis executives rate as human beings . . are they businessmen eyeing columns of figures and statistics, or arc they men who would gladly take time to come and sit with you and help you where they could if your wife were critically ill? The answer could well come from these descriptions:

Reg Merridew and his wife are lifelong church people; to them the first Kiwanis Object is a way of life. Reg says, "If I tried all day I couldn't phrase my personal philosophy any better."

Merridew is a big man, with a ready smile, warm and friendly. He works hard and plays hard. He is a family man. He likes people . . and he likes Kiwanis and its work.

Larry Hapgood is a church man, too. Of his philosophy, Larry says, "It is dominated by a firm belief in a very personal religion. I find that the true Kiwanian is one who lives by the Golden Rule, and who finds in Kiwanis the heartwarming experience of putting his personal religion into daily practice." Larry has taught Sunday school for years, for both youths and adults.

He is a big man, too, with a genuine interest in people, and the ability, always, to listen to a problem and to help to solve it. He likes the fun things of life, and he likes his family and Kiwanis, and that makes him every bit a human being.

With two such men at the helm of Kiwanis—wisely chosen, fitted by temperament, experience, and desire to fulfill the jobs they hold—Kiwanis can look forward to steady, top-flight leadership for many years to come.

*   *   *

Now it is possible and not altogether unpleasant to poke fun at the typical Kiwanis meeting. It usually begins with a hubbub of hellos, handshaking, wisecracks and laughter. This takes place (typically) on the mezzanine floor of the town's leading hotel near one of the dining rooms, or near the entrance to the Fellowship Hall of a local church. An aroma of coffee and creamed chicken pervades, and this serves, like the weather, as a conversation opener. Hungry males are gathering. They want to josh each other a bit, then eat.

That preliminary fifteen minutes may be the most valuable part of the whole session. For it is there that tensions can be ended, minds and muscles relaxed, troubles pushed away or into the background. A man can act boyish again. He can talk loud without self-consciousness. He can grab some lapels, slap some backs, poke some ribs, and get the same treatment for himself. He can tell The Boys that devastating New One he heard yesterday and know he will be appreciated with resounding laughter.

Laughter. In that alone, no matter how it is generated, is an alchemy of the spirit. Some astute club leaders have so recognized that fact as to *plant* skilled wisecrack artists and story tellers, a private committee that functions only in this pre-dining period. Laughter and let-down and friendliness—the things that a business man often needs most.

Virtually all clubs open their meetings with the singing of one verse of a song. *America,* though not the National Anthem, is most popular in the United States, just as its musical counterpart *God Save The Queen,* is first in Canada. The Pledge To The Flag follows, then the invocation. That prayer is nearly always meaningful, and done most often by a layman rather than a minister.

The food is likely to be less than memorable and is eaten with speed. The club singing—if there is time for it—brings a warm glow to all members, or there may be a special entertainer. But the main item of every good meeting is the speaker of the day. His talk must be geared to masculine appeal, must be both important and arresting if possible. Usually it is.

Such, then, is the Kiwanis Club meeting that had taken half a century to develop. The visitor may see little that suggests Building or service to mankind. Truth is, of course, the *work* of Kiwanis takes place in committees, behind the scenes, in meetings other than this weekly session. One major development has been elimination of most club business from the weekly sessions. Nothing is more dull, for instance, than a conventional "committee report"—unless it is the reading of the "minutes of the last meeting." Kiwanis avoids such errors.

It is the club's board of directors that has developed as the real controlling body of Kiwanis. This board takes over the business, leaving the weekly meetings open for lively programming and fellowship. If a club is asked to endorse this or that project, it must clear with the board of directors first. This takes a burdensome responsibility off the club president, who is constantly courted by propagandists and benefit seekers.

*   *   *

By the year 1966 almost all informed and thinking men had come to feel that development of the service clubs in North America was the greatest ethical advance of this century. For a while, back yonder in the teen years, many earnest folk feared that Kiwanis, Rotary, Lions and other such groups were "trying to start a new religion." Such fears of course were preposterous. Actually, the service clubs were and still are simply an extension of the religious ideals.

Let it go on record here, once and forever, that Kiwanis strives only to activate the good intentions of good men. They do not compete with, they cooperate with, the churches, supporting them wholeheartedly in their spiritual aims.

Kiwanians who give thought to it soon realize that the two greatest words in the English language are—*compassion,* and *outreach.* The one says we must feel for the needs of others, must have a sensitivity for their yearnings, a sympathy for their woes. Then—even more important—the second word says we must do something about it.

In those two words are wrapped up the whole story of Christianity and of most other accepted religions.

In those two words are wrapped up the whole world-wide programming of Kiwanis.

This kind of thinking was taking root in Kiwanis from its very beginning. Now it is achieving a new intensity. The ideals are fixed, even if the methods are not. Psychiatric emphasis, for example, is now shifting from what goes on inside people, to what goes on *between* people—looking to the inescapable crush of human beings that we face, the population explosion. In just such manner each club is now approaching a widening path of service. Opportunity gets wider . . . wider . . . wider with every rising sun.

END